Thomas Hugo

The History of Taunton Priory in the County of Somerset

Thomas Hugo

The History of Taunton Priory in the County of Somerset

ISBN/EAN: 9783337326265

Printed in Europe, USA, Canada, Australia, Japan

Cover: Foto ©ninafisch / pixelio.de

More available books at **www.hansebooks.com**

THE HISTORY

OF

TAUNTON PRIORY,

IN

THE COUNTY OF SOMERSET.

BY

THOMAS HUGO, M.A., F.S.A., F.R.S.L., &c.,

TRUSTEE AND MEMBER OF THE COUNCIL OF THE LONDON AND
MIDDLESEX ARCHÆOLOGICAL SOCIETY;
HONORARY FELLOW OF THE GENEALOGICAL AND HISTORICAL SOCIETY OF
GREAT BRITAIN;
HONORARY MEMBER OF THE SOMERSET ARCHÆOLOGICAL AND
NATURAL HISTORY SOCIETY;
AND MEMBER OF VARIOUS OTHER LITERARY AND ARCHÆOLOGICAL
SOCIETIES, BRITISH AND FOREIGN.

LONDON: J. R. SMITH, SOHO SQUARE.
TAUNTON: F. MAY, HIGH STREET.
1860.

PREFACE.

I offer the following History of Taunton Priory first to archæological and historical readers in general, and next to the local resident in particular. While the former will thereby possess a new, and I trust not unacceptable, chapter in their collection of Monastic Annals, to the latter it will impart no inconsiderable an acquaintance with the vicissitudes of a place which must needs be associated in his mind with a feeling of sacred interest, and in relation to which very little—and that not of the most accurate kind—has hitherto been offered to his study. He will here observe step by step how for several hundred years his ancient Priory and its learned and saintly Rulers entered into the life of England, how from a single Patron it soon attracted numerous friends and rose to a pre-eminence of power, how it gave a tone to the Society that it directed, and a character to the Region that lay around it, and how at length the day of blasphemy arrived, and irreligion and avarice concluded what piety and liberality had begun.

It is my intention, as it will be seen, to add in the form of an Appendix the originals of the Documents quoted or referred to, almost all of which are unpublished; but, before doing this, I solicit the kindly aid of those who desire to favour the present attempt, especially by communicating to me such supplementary facts, references, or documents as they may have it in their power to impart. I do not imagine that any material additions to the details which will here be found can be discovered in our national repositories, whose stores I have endeavoured to exhaust; but it is possible that one or more of my local readers may be in possession of some scrap of information—which, how minute soever, will be truly valuable—some ancient deed, or interesting legend, or curious relic of the structure or things connected with it, which he would be willing to have chronicled, and I should be well pleased and most thankful to record.

When the sheets were printed off, it was discovered that a series of Additions and Corrections had been omitted from their intended places in the text. They will be found immediately subsequent to these introductory remarks; and the reader will have no difficulty in perusing them in connection with their context, by attending to the references carefully prefixed to each.

It may probably appear to some of my readers that in the pages which follow, as well as in other of my contributions to historical literature, I have invested the Monastic System and the men who exemplified it with too pleasing a garb, and that I have sketched a portrait in which fancy will luxuriate, rather than one which sober seriousness will accept as true. To this I can only answer that I have represented my facts and my actors as I found them. If I have arrived at a false estimate of their merits, it has assuredly resulted from no want of study, nor from any absence of care. One consideration, however, may explain the reason of the difference observable between the pictures which I have drawn and those of many who have been pleased to employ upon the same subjects a totally different colouring. I do not attempt to write mediæval history from modern sources or with modern partialities. Rather it is my endeavour to give as faithful a representation of the times which I seek to illustrate, as many years spent among their records, some considerable investigation into their ways and modes of thought, and much willing submission to the labour and attention which such researches necessarily involve, may enable me to offer. I should indeed be unworthy of the position which I have the honour to hold, and of the manifold means which I have the happiness to possess of arriving at and eliciting truth, were I to use such a position and such means for the elevation of any measure or thing which I conscientiously believe to have been evil. At the same time I have offered no opinion, nor have I advanced a question as to how far, or if at all, the Monastic System is applicable to the times in which we live. This would have been altogether foreign to my purpose. I have but endeavoured to exhibit it as it was—not as perfect, for nothing upon earth is so, but marvellously great and inimitably adapted to the ages in which it did its work—and also, with the truthfulness which becomes an historian, to try to disabuse my readers of those false impressions which it has been the too frequent aim of the moderns to create and instil. That such misdirection has in many instances been the result of ignorance as well as malice cannot be denied. Later writers have been content to copy from earlier, without the study of the originals to which they were morally bound to apply themselves; and hence the designedly false portrait which the sixteenth century delineated has been accepted by the nineteenth as a true and faithful likeness. It is high time that the wrong should be amended. For my own part, I repeat, my first object is the knowledge and promulgation of truth; and, if the discovery of it obliges me to relinquish some favourite opinions, and to surrender some conclusions once accepted as irrefragable, it shall not greatly disturb me, and still less shall it induce me to suppress its declaration and thus do violence to its sacred claim.

T. H.

5, *Finsbury Circus*,
   13*th March*, 1860.

ADDITIONS AND CORRECTIONS.

Page 3, *line* 3, *read* the generality of students.
Page 6, *line* 1, *read* Aisse
Page 6, *note* ||, *add* Appendix, No. V.
Page 7, *line* 3, *read* Lydyard
Page 8, *line* 19, *insert* In or about the year 1180, the Priory of Buckland was transferred to the Knights Hospitallers of S. John of Jerusalem; and of the Canons of that House three were received on their own petition into the Hospital at Clerkenwell, two into the Priory of Taunton, one into the Priory of Berlitz, and one into the Priory of S. Bartholomew in Smithfield.*

Page 8, *note* *, *read* Appendix, No. VI.
Page 15, *line* 25, *for* 8s. *read* 100s.
Page 15, *line* 30, *insert* Wythele, £3 6s. 8d.
Page 16, *line* 15, *insert* In a Perambulation of the Forest of Exmore, made on the 22nd of March, in the 26th year of Edward I., 1297-8, the Prior of Taunton is stated to hold the vill of Broggelesnole and Levecote, and the hamlets of Telchete and La Merse, with their woods, heaths, and other appurtenances. (See page 77.) †

Page 19, *line* 19, *add* Otterford, Withiel,

---

* MS. in Off. Armor. L. 17. Dugd. VI., 837. Appendix, No. CLXXIV.
† Ad. de Domerham, Hist. Glast. I., 193, 194. Appendix, No. CLVI.

Page 19, *line* 24, *read* 22nd of May,

Page 37, *line* 9, *insert* On the 5th of June, 1337, the 11th year of Edward III., Rauf [de Culmstock], Prior of Tanton, did homage and fealty to John de Beauchamp for lands in Capelonde (see page 15), in the presence of Roberd de Cuerdene, parson of Haicch, Johan de Marcys, Richard de Molyns, and others.*

Page 40, *line* 26, *read* March;

Page 40, *line* 28, *read* April,

Page 41, *line* 6, *add* In the licence to elect, the Bishop, after wishing the Sub-prior and Convent "health in the embraces of the Saviour," and acknowledging the receipt of the intelligence of the vacancy, and of their petition to elect a successor to their deceased Prior, beseeches them "in the name of Jesus Christ to have before their eyes in the election God alone and the common advantage of their House; and, putting away from them the vice of singularity and all carnal affections, and uniting each several heart in the bond of peace and concord, holding, according to the apostolic precept, the same sentiments, so that there be no schisms among them, to endeavour to choose for their prior and pastor a man pleasing to God, approved for the sincerity of his religion, peaceful and prudent, not a slave to unsuitable will, but more desirous of profiting his brethren than of preeminence over them, under whose vigilant care their monastery may be prosperously directed, and by the divine mercy be amply blessed."†

To this the Convent replied as follows:—"To the venerable Father in Christ, lord William, by the grace of God Bishop elect of Winchester, and confirmed Patron

* Beauchamp Cartulary, in Aug. Off. p. 64. Appendix, No. CLXXV.
† X Registr. Edyndon, tom. 1., fol. 8. Appendix, No. CLXXVI.

of the Conventual Church of Taunton, of the diocese of
Bath and Wells, his humble and devoted Chaplains and
Canons Regular, Robert Sub-prior and the Convent of the
said Church, in devoted humility of soul, with all the
reverence and honor due to so great a father, intimate to
your lordship, by the tenor of these presents, that, our
Church aforesaid being vacant by the death of brother
Robert de Messyngham, the last Prior of the same, and
licence having been conceded to us by your lordship of
electing a future Prior, all things having been observed
which by the law and custom of the Church are so to be,
we have elected for our Prior our beloved in Christ,
Brother Thomas Cook by name, one of our brethren and a
Canon of the aforesaid Church, a man provident and dis-
creet, the bearer of these presents. Hence it is that we
present the same to your lordship, supplicating with devout
entreaty that, affording your gracious assent to our aforesaid election, you would be pleased by the consideration of
charity to direct your letters to the venerable Father lord
Ralph [Radulphus de Salopia] by the grace of God Bishop
of Bath and Wells, our diocesan, upon this, and that the
said father would favourably condescend to perfect those
things which in regard to the dispatch of the said election
are incumbent on his pastoral office. May the Most High
long preserve your lordship for the rule of His holy Church.
Dated in our Chapter House at Taunton, on the last day
but one of the month of March, in the year of our Lord
MCCCXLVI."* The Bishop of Winchester in his letter to
his brother at Wells complies with this prayer, and, after
express mention of his licence having been obtained and
his assent given, desires his favour in behalf of the elect,

---

* E Registr. Edyndon, tom. I., fol. 10b. Appendix, No. CLXXVII.

whom he praises as a man allowed by report to be "richly endued with perfection of manners, sincerity of religion, and other gifts of grace." *

Page 41, *note* * *add* MS. Harl. 6965, p. 176.

Page 45, *line* 28, *read* November, 1361,

Page 45, *line* 29, *read* January, 1361-2,

Page 46, *line* 2, *add* The Bishop in both of these instruments uses very similar terms to those with which the reader has already been made acquainted, and in the former of them urgently presses upon the attention of the community the importance of the duty which had devolved upon it.†

Page 46, *line* 11, *insert* In a Perambulation between the Counties of Somerset and Devon, ordered to be made on the 1st of July, in the 41st year of Edward III., 1367, the Prior of Taunton was affirmed to hold a certain croft at the line of division, between a spring called Owiline (see page 15) and Payneshurne. The Perambulation was confirmed by "inspeximus" by Richard II., on the 4th of February, 1385-6.‡

Page 47, *line* 28, *insert* On the 1st of July, 1382, John de Kyngesbury, Prior, and his Convent, proved in the Court of Chancery their right to the lands and advowson of the Church of Wildelond, or Willelond, in the County of Devon, an early gift of William Fitz-Odo. (See page 7.) The record is dated on the octave of S. John the Baptist, 6th Richard II., which is coincident with the date above given.‖

Page 48, *line* 14, *add* or S. Giles,

Page 48, *line* 20, *read* permit willows

* E. Registr. Edyndon, tom. 1., fol. 11. Appendix, No. CLXXVIII.
† Reg. Edyndon, tom. 1., ff. 112b, 113b. Appendix, No. CLXXIX.
‡ Pat. 9 Ric. II., p. 2, mm. 32, 33. Appendix, No. CLXXX.
‖ Inquis. p.m. 6 Ric. II., n. 174. Appendix, No. CLXXXI.

Page 51, *line* 8, *insert* On the 1st of April, 1403, a letter was addressed in the name of K. Henry IV. to various personages, requesting the loan of the sums specified against their names, to enable him to resist the Welch and Scotch. The amount thus solicited of "Le Priour de Taunton" was "v^e mares." *

Page 52, *note* ‡ *add* Reg. Well. Bowet, 48.

Page 53, *line* 14, *insert* At an Inquisition taken at Barnstaple, on the Wednesday after the feast of S. Lucia, Virgin, in the 4th of Henry VI., or the 19th of December, 1425, before Thomas Beaumont, the King's Escheator, the Prior was stated to hold land in Lucote (see page 29) at half a knight's fee, of the clear yearly value of two shillings beyond all reprises.†

Page 53, *line* 19, *read* Hullyng

Page 53, *line* 21, *insert* to Richard Marchaunt of Taunton, and John Baker, John Tanner, John Okham, Roger Touker, William Goky, William Payn, Thomas Oschern, and John Mavyell, of the same place,

Page 57, *line* 3, *read* 1475-6,

Page 57, *line* 31, *insert* the 7th of March,

Page 62, *line* 14, *read* Pytmynster

Page 64, *line* 25, *insert* On the 20th of May, 1524, Thomas Waren and John Mount conveyed to William Bury, Vicar of Taunton, John Swayne, clerk, Roger Hill, William Tedbury, John Soper, John Eston, Robert Horsey, and others, divers lands, tenements, and rents in Taunton, and elsewhere, bequeathed by John Bisshop in behalf of a chantry lately founded by him in the Church of S. Mary Magdalene.‡

* MS. Cott. Cleop. F. vi., f. 284. Proceedings of Privy Council, i., 201. Appendix, No. CLXXXII.

† Inquis. p.m. 4 Hen. VI., n. 32 (12). Appendix, No. CLXXXIII.

‡ Ex Original. in Off. Aug. L. 49. Appendix, No. CLXXXIV.

Page 73, *line* 29, *insert* occurs in 1337;

Page 74, *line* 9, *after* 1378; *insert* occurs in 1382;

Page 75, *line* 15, *add* In 1391, John Russchton was Sub-prior.

Page 76, *line* 9, *insert* William Moyhun, 1347;

Page 77, *line* 4, *read* Levecote

Page 80, *line* 17, *read* was

Page 85, *note* * *add* Claus. 26 Hen. VIII. m. 15. Rymer Fœd. XIV. 504.

Page 100, *line* 23, *insert* On the 15th of January, 26 Hen. VIII., 1535, the Prior William Wyllyams and Convent granted a corrody to John Wadham. By this and the instances which follow, we gain a very curious insight into the internal arrangements and life of the House, as well as a specimen of the heavy charges to which many of the greater monasteries were obliged to submit. The corrody consisted of regular maintenance, day by day and year by year during life, in eatables and drinkables for himself at the table of the Prior, "ad mensam Prioris," and for two servants at the table of the servitors, "ad mensam valectorum," or an equivalent if absent of two shillings a week; six acres of their meadow called Hole Mede, in their demesne lands, the produce of which to be cut and carried for the said John; a sufficient stable called the West Stable next to that commonly called the Gesten Stable; twelve bushels of beans and the same quantity of oats, or at his pleasure eight pence for each bushel of beans and six pence for each bushel of oats; pasturage for four horses all the year in their pasture called Carterlease; a sufficient chamber called the Toure Chamber in the chapel, with an inner chamber and all other appurtenances; sixteen cartloads of firewood from their demesne woods called the Moure; and four ells of cloth for his livery, "pro librario suo," of the value of six shillings an ell. In case of non-performance the Convent was to forfeit the sum of twenty shillings, for which the said John Wadham was empowered to distrain. The Court of Augmentation allowed the said John, in Michaelmas Term, on the 25th of October, 1539, instead of this corrody, the sum of seven pounds a year, with arrears from the dissolution of the House.*

On the 31st of December, 1537, the Prior and Convent granted by special favour an annual benevolence to William Grendon, vicar of Nynehed, and one of the Canons and brother of the House, consisting of a weekly delivery of eight conventual loaves and of eight flagons of conventual ale. In lieu of this the Augmentation Court allowed him on the 6th of February, 1541, an annuity of fifty shillings and arrears.†

On the 10th of February, 1538, the Prior and Convent granted to John Bytford, Bachelor of Arts, an annuity of five marcs sterling, issuing from the lands and tenements of their manor of Myddyldon, with power to distrain; maintenance in eatables and drinkables at the table of the Prior, and for his serving boy with the boys of the chapel; a sufficient chamber which one Roger Worthe aforetime had; wood for his fire in the aforesaid chamber, to be delivered every day at the door thereof; a white loaf and a quart of conventual ale every night, and two candles to be supplied for the said chamber, or wheresoever else it might please the said John; and four ells of woollen cloth " pro libario suo," of the value of five shillings per ell. This was given " for good service and diligence in teaching and instructing our novices and the whole Convent in the

* Enrolments of Orders and Decrees in the Exchequer, Off. Aug., vol. VI., f. clxxvii, clxxvii b. Appendix, No. CLXXXV.

† Enrolments, vol. VII., f. xxviii. Appendix, No. CLXXXVI.

rudiments of grammar and other kinds of literature." So much for monastic ignorance, on which it is too generally the fashion to dilate. Taunton Priory was in fact one of the schools in which knowledge exercised her sway, and John Bytford was her honoured teacher. The Court of Augmentation adjudged him, in lieu of this grant, an annuity of five pounds for life, with arrears, on the 17th of November, 1539.*

On the 25th of June, 1538, the Prior and Convent granted to John Cars the office of Bailiff of Dulverton, Buggethole, and Lewcote; a rent of three pounds sterling, issuing from their rents and tenements in Dulverton; ten cartloads of fuel, as much as four yoke of oxen could draw or carry from any of their woods in Dulverton, except Mershe Wood; and a robe or tunic of the livery of the said Prior and Convent, as the servitors of the said Prior and Convent have. He obtained in lieu of this from the Court of Augmentation, on the 10th of February, 1540, an annuity of four pounds with arrears.†

Shortly afterwards the Prior and Convent made a grant to another of their instructors. On the 16th of September, 1538, they agreed to give to Thomas Foxe, their organist and chapel master, an annual stipend of five pounds sterling, payable quarterly; four cartloads of fuel from their own woods, to be carted to his house at their expense; a house of theirs without fine next their tenement in Canon Street, at a rent of six shillings and eight pence; a gown or robe "ex librariis nostris optimis;" and maintenance daily at the table of the cellarer or with the servants "ad ultimam refectionem in aula." In return for this he was to teach and instruct the boys in the musical part of Divine

* Enrolments, vol. VI. ff. clxxxvii b, clxxxviii b. Appendix, No. CLXXXVII.
† Enrolments, vol. IV. f. 117. Appendix, No. CLXXXVIII.

Service daily in their chapel, and if any one of the Canons should be disposed to learn to play on the organ, the said Thomas was to instruct him to the best of his ability. The Augmentation Court ordered him in lieu thereof an annuity of five pounds for life, with arrears, on the 20th of June, 1539.*

On the 10th of December, 1538, they granted to John Tregonwell, Doctor of Laws, out of the special regard which they entertained for him, an annuity of three pounds charged on their manor of Dulverton. It would appear that this regard was founded rather on the hopes of future aid than on gratitude for services already received. In the present as in other instances, however, wherein we find this John Tregonwell mentioned in a similar manner, the hope was delusive, for he soon appears as one of the tyrant's agents in the suppression of the House. The annuity, therefore, was of course ordered by the Court of Augmentation to be paid, together with arrears, on the 10th of February, 1540.†

Five days subsequently, 15th of December, 1538, they granted to William Glastok, out of their special regard for him, an annuity, charged upon their manor of Wyllonde, of forty shillings, with power to distrain. The Court of Augmentation continued the annuity with the arrears, by an order dated the 12th of February, 1540.‡

It will be perceived that these details are derived from the Enrolments of Orders and Decrees in the Exchequer, where the grounds of each petition are severally stated as above. It is only too certain, however, that these Orders were but little regarded. The government grew weary of

---

* Enrolments, vol. x. f. iii^{e}xxiii b. Appendix, No. CLXXXIX.
† Enrolments, vol. iv., f. 199b. Appendix, No CXC.
‡ Enrolments, vol. iv., f. 4b. Appendix, No. CXCI.

the constantly recurring payments, and endeavoured to rid itself summarily of an irksome and vexatious burden.

I may here add, in completion of the subject, that the same Court of Augmentation ordered divers sums to be paid to the Dean and Chapter of Wells, the Chancellor of Wells, and the Archdeacons of Wells and Taunton, under the various heads of pensions, synodals, &c.;[*] and that on the 28th of May, 1543, it granted to Matthew Whytlyng, Chantry Priest of Donyatte (see pp. 37, 45, and 90), a decree for the continuance of his annual pension of £3 6s. 8d.[†]

Page 102, *line* 24, *add* He consecrated the Church and Cemetery of S. Saviour, at Puxton, on the Festival of the Conception, the 8th of December, 1539, and was presented to the prebend of Whitlakynton on the 4th of January, 1557-8.[‡]

Page 106, *note* *, *add* Reg. Well. Fuller, 314. MS. Harl. 701, f. 104b. MS. Lansd. 97, f. 6. Rymer, Fœd. xiv. 635.[∥]

Page 110, *line* 28, *instead of the extract from Willis, the names in whose lists are very often inaccurately given, insert,* There remained here in charge on the 24th of February, 1556, the following:—

Fees.	To John Wadham, chief steward, lxvjˢ viijᵈ
	To John Soper, auditor, lxvjˢ viijᵈ
Annuities.	To John Tregonwell, xlˢ
	To William Catlowe, clerk, xxxˢ
	To John Wadham, vijˡⁱ
	To Thomas Huishe, xlˢ
	To John Hodgeson, xlˢ
	To William Porteman, xlˢ
	To Sir Roger Bluet, xlˢ

---

[*] Enrolments, vol. iv., f. 9b.; vol. v., f. clxxxiii b.; vol. x., f. cccliiii; vol. xiv., f. clvhˢ b. Appendix, No. CXCII.

[†] Enrolments, vol. xiv. f. xxxxv b. Appendix, No. CXCIII.

[‡] MS. Harl. 6967, ff. 53b, 67b. Appendix, No. CXCIV.

[∥] Appendix, No. CXCV.

TAUNTON PRIORY.

	To Henry Seymor, xl^s
	To John Hethe, xxvj^s viij^d
	To Thomas Foxe, c^s
	To James Dier, xx^s
	To John Bitford, c^s
	To William Grenton, l^s
	To John Tregonwell, lx^s
	To William Glastoke, xl^s
PENSIONS.	To Nicholas Beram, vj^{li}
	To William Baylie, vj^{li} xiij^s iiij^d
	To John Warren, cvj^s viij^d
	To John Haywarde, cvj^s viij^d
	To John Cokeram, cvj^s viij^d
	To William Persons, cvj^s viij^d
	To William Brynesmede, cvj^s viij^d *

PENSIONS ALSO TO THE FOLLOWING CHANTRY PRIESTS:

    To William Callowe, last Incumbent of a Service in the Church of Westmonkton, lxvj^s viij^d †

    To Robert Gane, last Incumbent of a Chantry at Stafordell, of the foundation of Lord Zowche, c^s

    To Henry Bull, last Incumbent of S. Andrew's Chantry, Taunton, c^s

    To Ralph Wilkins, last Incumbent of Holy Trinity Chantry, c^s

    To William Callowe, last Incumbent of S. Etheldred's Chantry, c^s

    To John Seyman, last Incumbent of S. Michael's Chantry, iiij^{li} xvj^s

    To William Trowbridge, last Incumbent of the Fraternity, iiij^{li}

    To John Pytte, last Incumbent of B. Mary's Chantry, iiij^{li}

    To Alexander Maggot, last Incumbent of the Chantry called Swings Chauntry, lxxiiij^s iiij^d ‡

---

* Card. Pole's Pension Book, fol. xxix. Appendix, No. CXCVI.
  † Id. fol. xxx. Appendix, No. CXCVII.
  ‡ Id. fol. xxxj. Appendix, No. CXCVIII.

Page 124, *line* 27, *insert* The Requests to purchase and Particulars for this and the following grants are in the Augmentation Office. William Chaplyn and John Selwood's Request to purchase is dated 1st March, 36 Hen. VIII.*

Page 124, *note* *, *add* Particulars for Grants, in Off. Aug. Add. MS. Brit. Mus. 21,307. p. 75. Wood Sales, Rot. 36, Hen. VIII. fol. 41. Rot. 37. f. 43.†

Page 125, *line* 1, *insert* The Request, &c. is dated 13th December, 36 Hen. VIII.‡

Page 125, *line* 15, *insert* To Lawrence Hyde a tenement belonging to Swing's Chantry, a Chantry House and burgages belonging to S. Andrew's Chantry, a Chantry House and other tenements belonging to Swing's Chantry, all in the Church of S. Mary Magdalene, and Nethweys Chapell belonging to S. Etheldrede's Chantry.§ To John Dodington a house belonging to a Chantry, also in the Church of S. Mary Magdalene.‖ To Giles Kelway and William Leonard rents of the Guild of the Holy Sepulchre, and of Trinity Chantry in the same Church.¶ And to William Twisden and John Browne a house and the rents of divers burgages belonging to Blessed Virgin Mary's or Bisshoppes Chantry in the same Church.**

T. H.

* Appendix, No. CXCIX.
† Appendix, No. CC. ‡ Appendix, No. CCI.
§ Particulars of Sales, vol. I., pp. 11b, 71b; vol. II., p. 198b. Add. MS. B.M., 21,314, pp. 172, 173, 175. Appendix, No. CCII.
‖ Particulars of Sales, vol. I, p. 40b. Appendix, No. CCIII.
¶ Id. vol. I., pp. 247b, 249. Appendix, No. CCIV.
** Id. vol. II., pp. 280b, 281, 281b. Appendix, No. CCV.

Taunton Priory.

JUST outside the eastern boundary of the town of Taunton, within sight of its towers and sound of its melodious bells, a number of green and flowery fields edge the winding banks of a river, than which not one in England presents more captivating scenes of peaceful retirement and rural beauty. The meadow next adjacent to the gardens, which belong to houses whose fronts are in the neighbouring street, yet exhibits features indicative of an use widely contrasting with that to which it is at present applied. Numerous inequalities of surface, although covered with a rich and luxuriant sward, unmistakeably suggest, even by their very regularity, the conclusion that the place has witnessed a far other and busier kind of life, whatever and whenever that was, than the existence of dreamy silence and uninterrupted repose to which it has been at length consigned. These grassy mounds, if they could reveal their history, might disclose to us many a tale of passionate interest, now, spite of all our care, kept secret from the world for ever, and buried beyond all power of recovery in the absorbing grave of time.

A stately Priory occupied the spot and made it holy ground. Its pious founder was blessed with the instinctive acumen of most similar benefactors, and selected his site with a taste and ability that left no cause for subsequent regret. From the very walls of the House the meadows sloped away gently towards the Tone; and the scene which stretched beyond was as lovely as any on which an Englishman's eye could rest. The valley in the foreground, through which the river winded, was all but a forest, though nominally devoted to the operations of the husbandman. Here the mill of Tobrigge was a conspicuous object, and behind it rose the groves of Hestercombe and the grey tower of Monkton. A little to the right, smiling in mysterious grandeur, was Creechbury Hill that looked down upon Bathpool and its noted mills. While the background of the picture was composed of the long and diversified line of the Quantocks, with Cothelstone, Buncombe, Woodball, and Burlinch * for their highest and most prominent points.

In addition to its special interest, as a locality consecrated by olden memories, the scene has many and peculiar charms for me. I have, therefore, most willingly undertaken some amount of pains and labour in endeavouring to collect and weave into a consecutive narrative the notices relating to this once celebrated House—including, as they necessarily must, the ecclesiastical history of the neighbourhood at large, of which it was the recognised head and

* Or Burlings.

canonical centre—which our various repositories of MSS. yet possess, and which, though existing in rolls and registers, are entirely lost to the world of students at large. A very few pages would be sufficient to contain the information, meagre in amount and with little pretensions to accuracy, which has hitherto been committed to the press; and I accordingly feel considerable pleasure that the result of my labours enables me to place before my reader a series of annals, which extend along a duration of several centuries, and, whether they refer to the donations of benefactors without or to the more private affairs of the House within, unite in furnishing him with a far clearer and more comprehensive knowledge of the subject of our present research than we have of most other establishments of a similar kind. To do this at last for Taunton Priory has indeed been a labour of reverential love, and is the only—yet withal, happily for me, precious—mode that I possess of showing alike my recollection of days and persons gone and past away, since the spot was first endeared to me, and my gratitude for the suggestion of many a good thought and high endeavour which the sacred locality has inspired,—influences whose power can never end save with the last moments of a life which they have not a little availed to colour.

Let my reader imagine himself seated on the fragrant sward, and think, as his eye travels over the rich and varied scene before him, that he is listening to what I have to communicate from the stores examined and collected for him from many a ponderous volume, thickly-written roll and faded charter, and placed at length in his secure possession.

The House derived its origin from the piety and munificence of William Gyffarde, Bishop of Winchester and

Chancellor of England, the "*Præsul incomparabilis*" of the *Historia major Wintoniensis*, some time (for the exact date is uncertain) about the year 1115, the 15th of King Henry I. It will be recollected that Taunton was a manor of the Bishops of Winchester;* and it is probable that this circumstance may have decided Gyffarde in the choice of his locality. Leland mentions his successor, Henry Bleasance, or de Blois, brother of King Stephen and grandson of the Conqueror, known as the princely benefactor of the hospital of S. Cross, near Winchester, and the unflinching friend of Archbishop Becket, as a joint founder.† Most likely the last-named bishop erected a portion of the Priory buildings, and from his liberality in this department was considered to deserve a share of the honour. To William Gyffarde, however, the merit of the original foundation is unquestionably due. The charter which commemorated the good work is not extant in any form; but the fact is certified by an Inquisition taken before the King's Eschaetor at Taunton, on the 6th of January, 1316-17, to which I shall draw the reader's attention in its chronological order. The House was founded for Black Canons, or Canons Regular, of the order of S. Augustine, (who had been first located by Eudo at Colchester in 1105, and the next year at S. Mary Overy in Southwark, by the same Bishop Gyffarde) and was dedicated to the Apostles SS. Peter and Paul.

The first contemporary notice which I have found relating to the Priory is contained in a charter by which Robert, Bp. of Bath, among the *notabilia* of his episcopate, converts Hywis, or Huish, part of his manor at Bane-

---

* Cod. Dipl. Ævi Sax. nn. MII., DXCVIIL, DC., &c. Domesday, vol. I., p. 87b. Rot. Hundred. 4 Edw. I, m. 13., &c.

† *Collect.*, vol. I., p. 81.

well, into a prebend in the Cathedral Church of Wells. The instrument * asserts that although the land in question, a hide in extent, as indeed its name implies, had been known of ancient times to be the property of the Church, it had been by the favour of the bishop's predecessors so transferred to the power and possession of many persons both clerical and lay, among whom were Walter de Moretan, Alfred, and Richard de Montacute, that it was in danger of being altogether alienated from its rightful ownership; and that therefore, to avoid any such mischance, it was released from its dangerous uncertainty of tenure, and constituted a perpetual prebend as aforesaid. The document bears date the 4th of November, 1159; and the witnesses—which, I may add, constitute a very valuable list, as more than one among them are the earliest superiors of their monasteries whose names have as yet been recovered—are Ivo, Dean of Wells, and his Convent; Peter, Prior of Bath, and his Convent; Alan, Abbat of Muchelney; Benedict, Abbat of Athelney; Robert, Prior of Glastonbury; William, Prior of Montacute; Stephen, Prior of Taunton; William, Prior of Bruton; and the Archdeacons Robert and Thomas. This is the earliest Prior in our list of those dignitaries, and the present is the earliest date at which he appears.

The same Stephen, together with his fraternity, made to Reginald, Bp. of Bath, who governed that see from the year 1174 to 1191, various concessions of episcopal dues in respect of their churches and chapels, with express reservation, however, of the chapels of S. James, S. George de Fonte (Wilton), S. Margaret's hospital chapel (near the almshouse beyond the East-reach turnpike-gate), and S. Peter de Castello (a chapel in the Castle). Similar con-

* MS. Harl. 6969, pp. 24, 25. See Appendix, No. I.

cessions were made in respect of their churches of Asse
and Wircle.* Stephen is also a witness to a charter of
Oliver de Dinan, recounting the gift of his church of
Bokelande,† and to one of Richard, Bishop of Winchester,
setting forth the gift of William lord of Haselburg of his
church of Haselburg, for conversion into prebends in the
Cathedral Church of Wells.‡ The latter is dated A.D.
1174. The same Prior occurs also in 1189. |

The Priory immediately upon its foundation was possessed of powerful friends, and soon became a wealthy and
flourishing community. In the reign of Henry the Second
the Canons obtained a charter of confirmation of the
several grants made to them by various benefactors from
their founder downwards. The charter itself does not
exist, but its several provisions are inserted and confirmed
in another, technically called a charter of "*Inspeximus*,"
of the 8th year of Edward III, which will presently be
noticed at length.

This charter of Henry II. ran as follows:—" Henry,
King of England and duke of Normandy and Aquitaine, and earl of Anjou, to the archbishops, bishops,
abbats, earls, &c., and all his faithful subjects of England and Normandy, French and English, health. Know
ye that I have granted and confirmed for a perpetual
alms to God and the church of Tanton, and the Canons
there serving God, the donations which have been reasonably made to them. Of the gift of Bishop William, the
founder of the same church, all the churches of Tanton, together with their chapels and all their appurte-

* MS. Harl. 6068, p. 37. Appendix, No. II.
† MS. Harl. 6068, p. 83. Appendix, No. III.
‡ MS. Harl. 6068, p. 61. Appendix, No. IV.
| Archer, from Reg. Well. I. ff. 35, 60.

nances, and the land of Blakedon (Blackdown), and the church of Kingeston with its chapels and their appurtenances ; the church of Lydiard with its appurtenances, the church of Legh (Angersleigh) with its appurtenances, the church of Hill (Hill Bishop's or Bishop's Hull) with its appurtenances. Of the gift of Bishop Henry, the church of Pypemynstr (Pitminster), with its appurtenances and chapels. Of the gift of Robert Arundell, two hides of land at Aiss (Ash), and the church of the same vill with its appurtenances. Of the gift of William Fitz Otho, the land of Wildeland (Willand), and the church of the same vill with its appurtenances, by the concession of William, his grandson and heir, as their charter attests. Of the gift of William de Moioun, the land of Lydiart (Lydeard). Of the gift of Richard de Turberville, by the concession of Hugh his brother, the church of Dulverton and the land of Golialand. Of the gift of Roger Brito, the land of Uppecot. Of the gift of Baldwin de Cumbe, the land of More. Of the gift of Geoffrey Foliot, one virgate and a half in the land of Stanton. Of the gift of Osbert and Geoffrey de Hidon, the land of Middeldon. Of the gift of Baldwin de Cumbe, sixteen acres. Of the gift of Hugh de Flury, twenty acres of land in Hestercumbe. Wherefore I will and strictly charge that the aforesaid Canons do have and hold for a perpetual alms all these things aforesaid with all their appurtenances, in wood and plain, in meadows and pastures, in ways and paths, in waters and mills, in fairs and markets, in marshes and vivaries, in fisheries, inside the burg and outside, and in all places and in all things, with soc and sac, and toll, and team, and infangenethef, and all their other liberties, and free customs and quittances. As well, and in peace, and freely, and quietly, and entirely,

and fully, and honorably as they have been reasonably
given to them, and as the charters of their donors attest
and confirm. Because they and all their possessions and
things are in my proper hand and custody as my proper
alms, and it will displease me if any man do them injury
and contumely. Witnesses, Richard Bp. of London,
Nigel Bp. of Ely, and Robert Bp. of Lincoln, Thomas
[à Becket] chancellor, Robert Earl of Leicester, William
Earl of Gloucester, Henry de Essex constable, &c. Dated
at London."

We can obtain a very near approximation to the date of
this charter from the names of the witnesses appended to it.
It could not have been previous to 1157, for in that year
Thomas à Becket was made Chancellor, nor subsequent to
1161, in which died the second Richard Beaumes, Bishop
of London, both of whom are among them.

Such, then, were the possessions of the Priory in the
early part of the reign of Henry II.

Robert occurs Prior in a deed dated May, 1197.[*]

King John, in a charter dated the 17th of July, 1204,
gave to the Canons of Taunton the pasture of Kingeshull,
from Wulfeldesont to Hunteneswell, in free, pure, and
perpetual alms. This charter may be found on an ancient
roll under the title "*Cart. Antiq. Z. n.* 16." It also appears,
with a few verbal differences, on the Charter Roll of the
6th of John, m. 12. The date annexed is the same in
both, but the latter was apparently copied from the former.
As this is the oldest charter made in favour of the Priory
which we possess exactly in its original form, a literal
English translation may not be unacceptable :—

"John, by the grace of God, etc. Know ye that we, by
the consideration of divine love, and for the health of our

[*] Appendix, No. V.

soul, and of our ancestors and our heirs, have given and by our present charter have confirmed to God and the Church of the blessed Apostles Peter and Paul of Taunton, and to the Canons Regular there serving God, the pasture and the waste of Kingeshull from Wulfeldesont as far as Huntencswell, the pasture to wit and the waste which customarily paid to our farm of Sumerton sixteen pence per annum; to be held by the same Canons of us and of our heirs, for a free, pure and perpetual alms. Wherefore we will and straitly charge that the aforesaid Canons do have and hold the aforesaid pasture and waste well, and in peace, freely, and honorably, dischargedly, and quietly from all custom and secular exaction, as the charter which we made to them whilst we were Earl of Morton reasonably attests. Witness W. Earl of Salisbury, and more besides. Dated at Westminster, the 17th day of July, in the sixth year of our reign (1204)."*

We learn from the Testa de Nevill that this property was situated upon Quantock. In the record referred to the name is written "Kingeshill," and the land is stated to have been accustomed to pay yearly to the Exchequer in London the sum of sixteen pence.†

The Prior appears to have proved his right, against William de Prabulle, to one carucate of land with its appurtenances at Wudeham, some time in the same reign. The record, however, is fragmentary, and the exact date uncertain, but it was probably about the year 1204.‡

John, Prior of Taunton, who does not appear in the lists of Dugdale and Collinson, and therefore, as a matter of course, not in those of Savage and other copyists, was

---

* Cart. Antiq. Z. n. 16. Appendix, No. VII.
† Test. de Nev., p. 162. Appendix, No. VIII.
‡ Frag. Rec. incert. temp. Reg. Joh. rot. 3. in dorso. Abrev. Plac. p. 95. Appendix, No. IX.

witness to a confirmation by Savaricus to the Abbot and Convent of Muchelney of the great tithes of their Church of Somerton.* The other witnesses were Benedict, Abbat of Athelney; Durandus, Prior of Montacute; and Gilbert, Prior of Bruton. Savaricus was Bishop of Bath from A.D. 1192 to 1205.

The same John was a party in a Fine made at Winchester, on the Tuesday after Michaelmas, 1204, with the William de Praule just mentioned, who disclaimed all title to lands in Wodeham and Godesaltr, in the county of Devon.†

It may not be amiss to record that the Archdeacon of Taunton and his official held their court in the Church of S. Mary Magdalene, in the 28th year of King Henry III. 1244.‡

In the 39th year of Henry III., 1255, the Prior is stated to possess a due and service of two shillings, payable by Reginald of Bath on land in Radewell held by him of Henry de Penebrugg in soccage.‖ He was also returned as paying towards an Aid for a royal marriage the sum of five marcs, and as owing five more.§

The Patent Roll of the 3rd year of King Edward I. 1275, exhibits the Prior of Taunton as possessed of common of pasture in Oggesole, and of a certain watercourse in Asse Herbert and Asse Prior's.¶

The House had by this time been founded upwards of one hundred and fifty years, and had been steadily increasing in wealth and importance. Since the death, however,

* MS. Harl. 6968, pp. 5, 6. Ex magno lib. cart. &c. Appendix, No. X.
† Appendix, No. XI.
‡ Plac. In Com. Dors. &c. Anno Reg. Hen. III., XXVIII. Abbrev. Plac. p. 121. Appendix, No. XII.
‖ Inquis. p. m. 89 Hen. III. MS. Harl. 4120. Appendix, No. XIII.
§ Test. de Nevill, p. 163. Appendix, No. XIV.
¶ Pat. 3 Edw. I. m. 35. Appendix, No. XV.

of Bishop Henry de Blois, the successor of their founder, the society had not, so far as our researches have enabled us to discover, augmented or renovated their conventual buildings. With the year 1277 a movement was made in this direction, which, as we shall remark during our progress, extended its operations over more than half a century. There exists a letter of Walter Bronescombe, Bishop of Exeter, dated at Clyst, on the 13th of March in that year, addressed to the Archdeacons of Exeter and Totness, reminding them of the account to be given at the last day, and of the duty of anticipating that period by the performance of good works, setting forth that he had authorised the Questors, the bearers of the letter, to solicit the alms of the faithful in the diocese of Exeter for one year, towards the erection of the Conventual Church of the Priory of Taunton, and exhorting and urging them to aid the collectors to the utmost of their power both by word and deed. The missive furnishes us with the additional information that the good Canons had commenced their church in a style of great magnificence. Although it is probable that a considerable increase in their treasury was the result of this appeal, the expensive nature of the fabric necessitated, as we have already observed, the employment of a similar mode of collecting funds on several subsequent occasions.*

The Prior was affirmed to hold in villenage a messuage and an acre of land with its appurtenances, in the suburbs of Taunton, by the jurors at the assize before the Justices Itinerant held at Somerton, on the morrow of the Festival of the Ascension, in the 8th of Edward I, which is coincident with the 31st of May, 1280.†

* E Reg. Dom. Walt. Bronescombe, Exon. Ep., fol. 85b. Appendix, No. XVI.
† Plac. de Jur. et Ass. Somers. 8 Edw. I. m. 18. Appendix, No. XVII.

In the 18th year of Edward I, 1290, Philip de Thorlakeston gave to the Prior and Convent one messuage and six ferlings of land with their appurtenances in Thorlakeston (Thurloxton), and Richard de Portbury gave them one ferling of land with its appurtenances in Westowe. It may be interesting to the reader if I briefly describe the process by which such property was conveyed during the ages connected with our present research, and of which the instance before us furnishes an easily intelligible example. Its object was to protect from injury the rights and possessions both of sovereign and of subject. A petition was in the first place made to the king for licence to alienate lands which the law of mortmain made unalienable, or to possess any peculiar favour or privilege, as the case might be. A writ was thereupon addressed to the King's Escheator, or Sheriff of the county, commanding him to empannel a jury, and to take their verdict on the question whether the granting of such licence or privilege would be to the damage or prejudice of the king himself or of others. On the verdict being returned that there would be no such damage or prejudice, the king's letters patent were issued in behalf of the donor and receiver, empowering the one party to give and the other to accept the property or privilege which was the subject of solicitation.

In agreement with this usage, we have three documents preserved among the Records, of which the following are literal translations. First, there is the King's writ to the Sheriff:—

"Edward, by the grace of God King of England, Lord of Ireland and Duke of Aquitaine, to the Sheriff of Somerset health. We command you that by the oath of trusty and liege men of your Bailiwick, by whom the truth of the matter may be better known, you diligently enquire whether it be to the damage or prejudice of us or of others, if we concede to Philip de Thorlakeston that he have power to give and assign to our beloved in Christ the Prior and Convent of Taunton one messuage and six ferlings of land with its appurtenances in Thorlakeston, to be held by the said Prior and Convent and their successors for ever, or not. And if it be to the damage or prejudice of us or of others, then to what damage or prejudice of us, and to what damage or prejudice of others, and of whom, and of what sort, and in what way, and of whose fee that messuage and land be, and how many are the mesne men between us and the aforesaid Philip, and how much that messuage and land be worth a year in all outgoings. And that you send us without delay that Inquisition distinctly and fitly made under your seal and the seals of them by whom it shall have been made, and this writ. Witness myself at Westminster, the sixth day of May, in the eighteenth year of our reign." Indorsed :—" The Inquisition which by that writ has been made is to this writ attached." *

Then comes the verdict of the jury so assembled :—

"Inquisition made before the Sheriff by oath of Richard de Nywton, John de Marisco, Simon le Bret, Simon Michel, David le Vygur, Thomas Lambryth, James de Orcharde, John de Treberge, Luke Mody, John Wyion, Richard le Hare, and John de Develiz, who say upon their oath that if our lord the King should concede that Philip de Thurlockeston should have power to give and assign to the Prior and Convent of Tanton one messuage and six ferlings of land with the appurtenances in Thurlockeston, to be held by the said Prior and Convent and their successors for ever, it would not be to the damage or prejudice of

* Inquis. ad qd. dam. 18 Edw. I, n. 63. Appendix, No. XVIII.

the King nor of others; and they say that the aforesaid Philip holds that messuage and that land of the said Prior and Convent, and that the aforesaid messuage and land are of the fee of the said Prior, and that the aforesaid Prior holds them of John de Mohun, and the said John of our lord the King in capite. They say also that there are no more mesne men between our lord the King and the aforesaid Philip, and that that messuage and that land are worth twelve shillings a year in all outgoings. In testimony whereof the aforesaid Jurors have to this Inquisition affixed their seals." *

A similar precept was issued to the Sheriff in the case of Richard de Portbury, and a similar verdict returned.†

Then, lastly, we have the letters patent granting the petition :—

"For the Prior and Convent of Taunton concerning licence of receiving land, &c. The king to all, &c., health. Although by the common counsel of our realm we have provided that it be not lawful for religious or other men to enter upon the fee of any person, so that it may descend in mortmain without our licence and that of the chief lord of whom that thing is immediately held, wishful nevertheless to do a special act of grace to Philip de Thorlakeston, we have given him licence, so far as in us lies, that he have power to give and assign one messuage and six ferlings of land with appurtenances in Thorlakeston; and to Richard de Porbury, that he have power to give and assign one ferling of land with appurtenances in Westowe, to our beloved in Christ the Prior and Convent of Taunton, to be held by them and their successors for ever; and

---

* Inquis. ad q. d. 18 Edw. I., n. 63. Appendix, No. XIX.
† Inquis. ad q. d. 18 Edw. I., n. 64. Appendix, No. XX.

to the said Prior and Convent, that they have power to receive that messuage and land from the aforesaid Richard and Philip by the tenor of these presents we similarly grant special licence; being unwilling that the same Philip and Richard, or the aforesaid Prior and Convent, by reason of our statute upon this in anything be molested or put to trouble; reserving nevertheless to the chief lords of that fee the services thencefrom due and customary. In testimony whereof, &c. Witness the King, at Westminster, the twelfth day of July." *

In the year 1288, Pope Nicholas IV. granted the Tenths of all ecclesiastical benefices, which together with the First Fruits had for a long period been paid to the Roman See, to King Edward I. for six years, as a means of defraying the cost of a crusade. In order that the most might be made of the Pope's concession, a taxation was commenced in the same year, and not entirely finished until four years afterwards. In this most interesting and important record, according to which all taxes both to the Pope and the King were strictly regulated down to the time of the Valor of Henry VIII, the Priory is stated to be possessed of lands at Ewilline in Staunton and Middeldon, valued at £2 2s. 5d.; Willclond, £2 0s. 4d.; Upstrete, 15s.; Capelod in Coury, 15s.; Preston, near Mulverton, 10s.; Essy Prioris (Ash Priors), 8s.; Nydehyde, (Ninehead), £1 5s.; Westmonck (Westmonkton), 10s.; Lydiard S. Laurence, 20s.; Bruges (Bridgwater), 10s.; Northperton, 20s.; Thornlockeston (Thurloxton), appropriated to the pitancier, £3 10s. 8d.; Spaxton, 13s. 4d.; Stregeston (Stringston), 9s.; Haswylle, 10s.; Dulvertone, also as it seems appropriated to the pitancier, 26s.; Toulonde, £1 11s. 3d.; and Stoke, £1 10s.

* Pat. 18 Edw. I, m. 18. Appendix, No. XXI.

The rectory of S. Mary Magdalene, with its chapels, was valued at the same time at £60; Pyministr, at £21 6s. 8d.; Nienhid, at £4 6s. 8d.; Kyngeston, at £13 6s. 8d.; Cumbeflori, at £4 1s. 8d.; Moncketon, at £20; Thurleber, at £6 13s. 4d.; Lidiard S. Laurence, at £9 6s. 8d.; and Esse Prior at £1. The Prior is returned as having a particular yearly pension from Dulverton of £3, and from Lidiard S. Laurence of £1 6s. 8d.*

In 1295, the Prior is stated to hold the vill of Wildeland, by a quarter of one knight's fee, of John de Humfraville, who held it of the king in capite.†

In the 25th of Edward I, 1297, the Prior is returned in the Parliamentary writs for the counties of Somerset and Dorset, as holding lands, &c., and similarly in 1300.‡

On the 6th of November, 1308, the 2nd year of Edward II., the chapel of S. Mary Magdalene at Taunton was constituted a vicarage. It had previously been served by the Canons of the Priory Church, who continued to be the rectors until the dissolution. The Ordination was made at Taunton, by Antony de Bradeneye and Henry de Chanyngton, Archdeacon of Taunton, the Commissioners appointed by the Bishop for that purpose, on the Tuesday after the feast of All Saints, Nov. 6th, and was confirmed by the Bishop on the Wednesday after the feast of S. Martin, Nov. 14th, in the year above mentioned. Walter Haselshaw was at that time Bishop of Bath and Wells, being elected in 1302 and dying in 1312. I have transcribed the document from the copy which exists among Dr. Hutton's extracts from the Wells Registers, made by him in the seventeenth century, and preserved among his MSS. in the British Museum;

---

* Tax. Eccl. P. Nich. IV., pp. 152, 183b, 198b, 204, 204b, 205, 205b. Appendix, No. XXII.
† Appendix, No. XXIII.   ‡ Parl. Writs, I., 858. Appendix, No. XXIV.

and, as it is one of more than ordinary interest for the general reader, a literal translation may not be unacceptable.

"Walter, Bishop of Bath and Wells, ordains and appoints that Master Simon de Lym, vicar of the chapel of S. Mary Magdalene, Tanton, the parish church appropriated to the Priory of SS. Peter and Paul at Tanton, as vicar incumbent and instituted in the same, shall every week in the year receive twenty-one canonical loaves, and forty-two conventual flagons of ale, and seven loaves, that is to say of boulted flour, of the same weight as the canonical loaves, and two loaves of finest white bread, and seven flagons of best ale; and shall receive every year of the said Prior and Convent fifteen marcs of silver; and six cartloads of hay, and seven bushels of oats every week for his horse, and two shillings for the shoeing of his horse every year; and shall receive freely all legacies made to him in the parish; and have the same houses and curtilages as those belonging to his predecessors, with the following cure and charge; namely, that he shall serve at his own cost, by himself and his curates, the chapel of S. Mary Magdalene of Tanton, of Trendle (Trull), of the Castle, and of Fons S. George (Wilton), in the sacraments and other Divine offices of the church; with this addition, that he shall find a priest constantly resident for the service at Trendle. Also we ordain that for the aid of the said vicar and his successors, to whom the cure of souls of the whole parish of the said parish church is specially committed by the ordinary of the place, and on whom it falls, the said Prior and his successors shall perpetually provide for himself and his successors for the performance of Divine service by one secular priest for the chapels of Stoke and of Riston (Ruishton) which are sufficiently contiguous, and

c

for the chapels of Stapelgrave (Staplegrove) and S. James by another secular priest, and also for the chapel of Hulle Bishop's by a third secular priest, each constantly resident in the said places, and with his own proper stipend; with this reservation, that the said Prior may cause service to be performed in the chapel of S. George of Ryston, and of S. James, on Sundays and holidays by some well-reputed of his brethren, with the license of the bishop, in assistance of the priests in masses, at least when need shall require. Also we ordain that the said vicar and all his priests serving in the said chapels do make oath of fidelity to the said Prior and rector at their admission, that they will repay and refund all and singular offerings in the aforesaid places to the Prior himself without trouble and defalcation. Also we will that for the augmentation of the said vicar's portions two quarters of corn shall be delivered to the said vicar from the grange or granary of the Priory at the festival of our Lord's Nativity. The ordinary charges more fully incumbent on the said parish church the aforesaid religious shall duly sustain, and their portion of the extraordinary according to the rating of the same. And the said Prior and Convent shall provide books, vestments, and other ecclesiastical furniture meet for the said chapels at their own expense. Dated at Tanton, Nov. 1308." *

In 1313 John is named as Prior. He was at that time very old and infirm, and the bishop appointed two of the Canons to be his coadjutors.† He is referred to, I presume, in the charter of the 8th of Edward III., to be noticed presently, as receiving land at Dulverton and Pleyston of Richard de Weteden. On the 2nd of April,

* MS. Harl. 6964, pp. 22, 23, 24. Appendix, No. XXV.
† Archer, from *Reg. Drok.*, f. 140. Appendix, No. XXVI.

1314, he gave consent, by Thomas de Sutton, Canon, to some contemplated amendments in the Ordination of the vicarage just noticed, which were not, however, carried into effect.*

We now arrive at another class of documents illustrative of the progress of the House and the exercise of its rights. We have already seen the Canons possessed of various appropriated rectories, and have now to regard them as patrons of the benefices thus committed to their rule. These notices will furnish us for upwards of two centuries with as complete a history as can now be recovered of the ecclesiastical changes in each of their parishes. As affording such information I hardly need say that they are of special interest and importance.

It may be as well, however, to enumerate the benefices which the documents already quoted mention as belonging to them. They were the churches of Taunton, (I give them in modern orthography) Bishop's Hull, Kingston, Lydiard S. Lawrence, Angersleigh, Pitminster, Thurlbeer, Ash Priors, Dulverton, Runnington, Combflory, Ninehead, Thurloxton, Willand, and Clannaborough. It must be recollected that S. James' in Taunton, Ruishton, Stoke S. Mary, Staplegrove, Wilton, and Trull, were chapels under Taunton.

On the 21st of June, 1315, Richard le Bellringer was presented by the Prior and Convent to the vicarage of Nyenhide.†

On the 8th of September, 1315, the Bishop certified the Treasurer and Barons of the Exchequer, that the Abbats of Glastonbury and Muchelney, and the Priors of Taunton and Montacute, had received for the maintenance of four Templars doing penance in their monasteries, for two

---

* Appendix, No. XXVII.
† MS. Harl., 6964, p. 26. Appendix, No. XXVIII.

hundred and seventy six days, at the rate of four pence a day for each.*

On the 5th of March, 1316, the 9th of Edward II., the Prior of Taunton was certified, pursuant to writ then tested at Clipston, as Lord of the Townships of Willand, Prior Merston, and Monksbeare, in the county of Devon. He was also certified in like manner, and at the same time, as one of the Lords of the Township of Dulverton.†

We now arrive at the formal proof of the identity of William Gyffarde and the founder of the Priory. This, as I have already stated, is contained in an Inquisition taken before the King's Eschaetor on the 6th of January, in the tenth year of K. Edward II., or A.D. 1316-7. The original, although one of the very few records belonging to this House which have hitherto been committed to the press, is given but in abstract, and with the omission of details always interesting to a local enquirer. A translation here follows for those of my readers to whom, in its native dress, it might not be familiar:—

"An Inquisition taken before the Eschaetor of our Lord the King, at Taunton, on the 6th day of January, in the tenth year of the reign of K. Edward; whether, to wit, the Priory of Taunton is of the foundation of the progenitors of our lord the king, some time kings of England, or of the progenitor of the king himself, or of others, or of another, and of what men, and of what man, and about what lands and tenements, and from what time: by the oath of John Horcherd, Philip de Bampton, John Aunger, John de Loveton, Geoffrey de Netherecote, William Punchardoun, William de Webbewelle, John

* MS. Harl., 6964, pp. 28, 29. Appendix, No. XXIX.
† Parl. Writs, vol. 11, div. 3, p. 387. Appendix, No. XXX.

Hywhys, William de Combe, Hugh de Reigny, Walter atte Walle, and William de Haleswelle. Who say upon their oath that the Priory of Taunton is not of the foundation of the progenitors of our lord the king, kings of England, or of the progenitor of some one king. But they say that the aforesaid Priory is of the foundation of one William Gyffard, formerly Bishop of Winchester, before the time of King Edmund Iryneside, from which time memory is not extant, of all his land in the northern part outside the east gate of his vill of Taunton, for the erection in the same place of a monastery, and its site by bounds and divisions contained and named in the charter of the same Bishop, for a pure and perpetual alms ; which very foundation and gift Henry King of England and Duke of Normandy and Aquitaine and Earl of Anjou confirmed by his own charter for a pure and perpetual alms, as in the charter of the aforesaid Bishop touching the aforesaid foundation and gift is more fully contained. And they say that the said Priory hath no lands or tenements of the foundation or gift of any progenitor whomsoever of the King of England, or of the progenitors of any whomsoever of the Kings of England. In witness whereof the aforesaid Jurors have to this Inquisition affixed their seals."*

The attribution by the Jurors of Bishop Gyffarde, who is known to have been consecrated in the year 1107, to a period anterior to that of King Edmund Ironside, although properly characterized by Dugdale as "error maximus," is nevertheless in some measure to be understood and accounted for. For, although the historians of the Anglo-Saxon æra are silent on the subject, there is

* Inquis. ad q. d., 10 Edw. II., n. 172. Appendix, No. XXXI.

abundant reason to feel assured that a monastic establishment existed at Taunton for a century and a half at least before the Norman invasion. Where their House was situated, whether on the site of the subsequent Priory or elsewhere, we have no means of discovering. But the fact of the existence of such a community does not admit of doubt. There is a charter of Bishop Denewulf to King Eadweard of Wessex, and a counter charter of the king to him, dated in the year 904,* "pro perpetua libertate illius monasterii quod dicitur Tantun," and speaking of it not as a new foundation, but as one which had existed for some considerable time. The bishop gives to the king certain lands at Stoce for this privilege. Among other customary liabilities due from the monastery, are enumerated board and lodging to the king for one night; the same for eight dogs and their keeper; for nine nights to the king's falconers; attendance, horses, carts, &c., when the king was progressing to "Curig" or "Willettun," together with attendance on the king's visitors to the nearest of his royal residences. It is probable that some confused tradition of such an establishment operated on the Jurors' minds in leading them to the conclusion, erroneous so far as the date, at which they arrived.

The proof of the correct attribution of the foundation of the Priory to Bishop Gyffarde, whatever may be the history or wherever the site of any earlier establishment, is by this Inquisition rendered doubly clear and conclusive. The reader will recollect that the document has been reserved until now, in order that it might occupy its exact place in the chronological series, although it refers to the earliest fact in the annals of the House.

---

* Cod. Dipl. Ævi Sax., nn. MLXXXII, MLXXXIV. Appendix, No. XXXII.

The thread of the narrative shall now be resumed.

On the 27th of September, 1317, the Prior and Convent presented John de Kingesbury to the church of Comflory.*

On the 30th of May, 1318, the Prior and Convent presented William de la Pytte to the church of Tholokeston.†

On the 4th of November, in the same year, they presented J. de Kyngesbury to the church of Lidiard S. Laurence, void by the resignation of Thomas de Columbrugg; and on the same day Thomas de Columbrugg to the church of Comflory, by exchange.‡

In January, 1321-2, the rectors, vicars, and other ecclesiastical persons in the Deanery of Taunton, gave of their own free will one penny in the pound of their incomes, according to the taxation of their benefices, towards the erection of a new bell tower in the Cathedral Church of Wells.‖

In December, 1325, died Prior Stephen de Picoteston; and Ralph de Colmstoke was elected Prior on the 6th of January, 1325-6, received assent on the 11th, and was confirmed in his office on the 23rd of the same month.§

The acceptance of the Prior elect and consent of the patron are thus recorded:—

"To the venerable Father in Christ Lord John, by the grace of God Bishop of Bath and Wells, John, by permission of the same, Bishop of Winchester, health and continual increase of mutual brotherhood in the Lord. The Conventual Church of blessed Peter of Taunton, of your diocese and our patronage, being lately vacant by the death

---

* MS. Harl. 6964, p. 56. Appendix, No. XXXIII.
† MS. Harl. 6964, p. 2. Appendix, No. XXXIV.
‡ MS. Harl. 6964, p. 5. Appendix, No. XXXV.
‖ MS. Harl. 6968, p. 109. Appendix, No. XXXVI.
§ MS. Harl. 6964, p. 99. Dr. Archer, from Reg. Drok., 270. Appendix, No. XXXVII.

of Lord Stephen de Pykouteston, the last Prior of the
same, and licence of electing a Prior having been asked for
and obtained of us the patron of the same church, Brother
Robert de Lym, Canon and precentor of the aforesaid
Conventual Church, and the Convent of the same place
have elected, as we have been certified, Brother Ralph de
Culmpstok, one of the Canons and sub-prior of the aforesaid Church, for the Prior and pastor of them and of that
Conventual Church. Wherefore we, so far as to us
belongs, accepting the person of him elected, presented to
us the patron of the same Church by Brothers Roger
Terry and William de Reygin, Canons of the said Church,
have given to his election our consent as well as our
assent. In witness whereof, &c. Given at Waltham, the
11th day of January, in the year of our Lord above
stated (1325-6), and of our consecration the third." *

On the 26th of August, 1326, William Syward was
presented to the church of Ronyngton, void by the death
of William de Lydeford.†

On the 8th of May, 1327, Richard de Fifhide was
presented to Hauckewell, void by the resignation of John
Broun.‡

We have already seen that, so early as the year 1277,
the Canons were commencing the erection of their Con-

---

* E Reg. Dom. Joh. de Stratford, Winton. Ep., fol. 13b. Appendix,
No. XXXVIII. I feel much pleasure in offering my grateful thanks to
the Rev. Dr. Oliver, for a complete copy of this document from the Winchester Registry, instead of the reference and abstract which I previously
possessed. To the same gentleman, the truly learned and accomplished author
of the *Monasticon Dioecesis Exoniensis*, I am likewise indebted for a copy of
the Indulgence granted in 1472, in behalf of S. Margaret's hospital, noticed
at a future page, and for a complete copy of the Petition of the Convent to
the Patron for leave to elect a Prior on the resignation of John Prous,
dated the 3rd of February, 1513-4, both also from the Winchester Registry.

† MS. Harl. 6964, p. 105. Appendix, No. XXXIX.

‡ MS. Harl. 6964, p. 106. Appendix, No. XL.

ventual Church in a style of sumptuous magnificence. Fifty years had elapsed from that period, and the fabric was still unfinished; not so much perhaps from failure of the appeal then issued as from the expensive and onerous nature of the work itself. An attempt, however, was now made to bring it to a conclusion, and funds were collected by the instrumentality of an Indulgence. John de Stratford, Bishop of Winchester, who appears to have been not only the ecclesiastical patron but the firm and munificent friend of the Priory, issued a letter "to our beloved sons, our Archdeacons of Winchester and Surrey and their officials, and deans, rectors also and vicars and parish chaplains both exempt and non-exempt within our diocese, health, grace, and benediction." He reminds them of the value to the souls of Christian people of alms expended in the erection of sacred edifices, and then introduces to them the object of the present appeal, the completion of the Conventual Church of Taunton lately commenced, which was now unhappily delayed through lack of funds. He enjoins and commands them, when the messengers or procurators made their appearance, to receive them with all kindness, to stir up their people to a work of so great piety and charity, and to do their best, both in their own persons and in those of their flocks, to make the mission of the collectors effectual. And, in order to incite them to this duty, he concludes by granting to all those who with contrition and confession shall give aid to the good work an Indulgence of forty days. "In testimony whereof we have ordered our seal to be affixed to these our letters patent, to last for two years from the present date. Dated at Rympton, the 30th of September, in the year of our Lord one thousand three hundred and twenty seven." *

* E Reg. Dom. Joh. de Stratford, Winton. Ep., fol. 20. Appendix, No. XLI.

In 1330, the Prior was one of the sub-collectors of the tenth demanded by the Pope, to be divided equally between himself and Edward III. The other sub-collectors were the Abbats of Glastonbury and Keynesham.*

In the same year the Prior was affirmed to hold of John de Mohun (*see page* 14) the manor of Thurloxton, by the service of one knight's fee.†

On the 4th of December, 1331, the Bishop dates at Taunton a letter for a subsidy in behalf of the completion of a chapel by Pontefract Bridge, Yorkshire.‡

On the 9th of March, 1331-2, a commission is given to Ralph the Prior to wash with holy water the Conventual Church, which had incurred pollution "by the shedding of blood."‖

On the 20th of March, 1332, the Prior and Convent presented Richard de Poterne to the vicarage of Tanton; and on the 2nd of September, in the same year, the Prior was summoned to the council in London, together with the Abbats of Glastonbury, Muchelney, Athelney, &c. Thomas Flour of Southpedertone was, on the 24th of the same month, presented to the vicarage of Dulverton, on the death of Adam, late vicar thereof.§

On the 26th of July, 1333, Walter de Quenton was presented to the church of Thurlokeston, on the resignation of Gilbert.¶

I have now to present the reader with one of the most precious documents which we possess in connexion with the House, but one whose value has nevertheless been very

---

* MS. Harl. 6965, p. 35. Appendix, No. XLII.
† Inquis. p. m. 4 Edw. III. n. 35. Appendix, No. XLII. (2).
‡ MS. Harl. 6965, p. 40. Appendix, No. XLIII.
‖ MS. Harl. 6965, p. 54. Reg. Well. Rad. 51. Appendix, No. XLIV.
§ MS. Harl. 6965, pp. 67, 62, 63. Appendix, No. XLV.
¶ MS. Harl. 6965, p. 78. Appendix, No. XLVI.

much overlooked. The charter to which I refer, which is one of "*Inspeximus*," was granted in the 8th year of K. Edward III., and bears date the 1st of October, 1334.* It is a document of considerable length, occupying a large portion of two membranes of the venerable roll in which it is contained, and extending to two hundred and ten lines of closely penned and much abbreviated writing. I have, however, willingly undergone the labour of transcribing it, on account of its paramount importance in the history of the Priory. Dugdale contented himself with copying and publishing the first few lines only; and subsequent writers, no doubt supposing that he had given the whole, are characteristically silent with respect to the far more voluminous remainder. I shall, therefore, continue the list of donors and donations, as furnished by this most valuable and important record, giving the names of the localities—as I have done and shall do throughout this memoir—in their original orthography. Though so lengthy, it will be found to repay most richly a minute examination and an attentive study.

The first donation which occurs after those whereof mention is made in the charter of Henry II., is that of King John, with which the reader has been already presented, of the pasture of Kyngeshell from Wulfeldesont, or Wulfhefdyete, to Huntenewell. Then we have the gifts of Gilbert de Helleworth, of the advowson and church of Runeton; of Ralph de Flory, of a virgate of land called Beidun in Wideln; of Richard de Plessetis, lord of Nyweton, of land called Chademede; of Richard de Montacute the younger, of an acre of land at Thorlebere, adjoining a place called Therless; of William de Montacute, of the church of

* Cart. 8 Edw. III., n. 12, mm. 5, 6.   Appendix, No. XLVII.

Thurlebere; of Simon de Montacute, son and heir of William, of the advowson of the church of Thorlebere; of the same Simon, of a confirmation of all donations granted by his ancestors; of the same, of an acquittance with respect to the enclosure of the park of Donneyhete; the gift of the same, of four quarters and five bushels and a half of corn, from his granary at Thurlebere, every year on the festival of S. Martin; of William de Montacute, of that portion of land at Thurlasse which his mother had previously given; of Walter, son and heir of Bernard de Pereton, of lands at Northpereton and Neweton, with their liberties, customs, and dues; of Henry de Erlegh, of fines, &c., connected with the said lands; of the same, of an acquittance of various dues, including that of a yearly rent of eighteen pence received by him from the land of Colemanneshat; of the same Henry, of fifteen acres of land in his moor of Northmore; of the same, of free ingress to and egress from, and liberty to repair a trench in the aforesaid land; of Reginald, son and heir of Jordan de Pykeston, of his land at Pykeston; of William de Pykeston, son of Jordan de Pykeston, of his land at Pykeston and Linegereslaund; of Robert Feroun, of land held by him of the fee of Wolmarestone; of Baldewin Fitzgirold, of land called Lynyegereslaunde at Nygahide; of Robert Feroun, of land in Eeshe; of the same, of one messuage with two gardens in Mulverton; of Simon de Flury, son and heir of Hugh de Flury, of forty acres in his manor of Cumbe; of the same, of sixteen acres in his manor of Cumbe; of the same, of nine acres and a half in his manor of Cumbe, in the land called Galand; of the same, of the church of Lydeard S. Laurence with all its appurtenances, and of the church of Cumbe with its appurtenances and liberties; of Ralph de Flury, of thirty two acres beyond the ancient trench of Guppewurve, and of common of pasture in the whole of his land towards the west, so far as the head of Guppewurve, &c.; of Cecilia, formerly wife of William de Mounceaux, of one ferling of land in the manor of Wyvele; of William Bret, of one virgate of land called la Grave, and of half a virgate called la Sale; of Andrew de Bovedon, of his land at Gaveldene; of Gilbert de Wypelesdene, of the gift of Andrew de Buhedon of his land of Gaveldon in Taland; of Cecilia Bozoun, formerly wife of Geoffrey de Lidyard, of the watercourse through her land in the manor of Taland; of Ralph Fitzurse, lord of Wyleton, of land at Brimeton for the formation of a head and other necessary adjuncts to the said watercourse; of Lucy, daughter of Simon Bozoun, of land in Talaunde; of Andrew de Boghedone, of half a virgate of land in Thalande, with a messuage, &c., which William de la Gerche held; of the same Andrew, of half a virgate of land and its appurtenances, one part of which lies in Lunedon and the other towards Lydyart Cross; of Ralph le Tort, of four ferlings of land in the manor of Wynemeresham, &c.; of Roginald le Tort, son of the aforesaid, of all his land of Luycote, and of all his wood of Chiddescumbe, of ground for the erection of a mill in Lytlecoumbe, of the watercourse of Luycote, of liberty in the moors belonging to Wynemeresham, of the wood of Luycote, the end of the wood of Yelescumbe, and ten hogs with free feed in the wood of Wynemeresham; of Ralph le Tort, of all his land of Luycote; of the same, of the liberties pertaining to the manor of Wynemeresham; of Richard de Wrotham, of all his land at Luycote with all its appurtenances; of Peter Giffard, son and heir of Peter Giffard, of a rent of twenty shillings which he received of the land of Hupesterte, &c.; of Geoffrey, son and heir

of Philip de Luccumbe, of the land of Buggedehole, with
its appurtenances, liberties, and customs; of the same
Geoffrey, of thirty hogs with free feed in the woods of
the same Geoffrey; of William Fychet, of one ferling of
land in Merryg; of the same, of common of pasture; of
Gilbert, son of Hugh Fychet, of land which he held of the
gift of William, his brother, in Merygg; of William, son of
Engelisia de Merigge, of seven acres of land in Merygg;
of Hugh Fychett, of one virgate of land with all its appurtenances, and three men, Hugh son of Richard, and William
his brother, and John son of Selegine, in his manor of
Strengestun, and of common of pasture in all his land in
Strengiston; of Albrea, formerly wife of the aforesaid Hugh,
of the same land, men and pasture; of Robert Vaux, of one
ferling of land in Capilaunde, and nine acres next adjacent
to la Hokederewe, and of the whole land held aforetime by
Geoffrey Chaunterel, &c.; of the same Robert, of twenty
hogs and one boar free of feed yearly in the wood of Capi-
lande, called la Yornete; of Henry de Orchiat, of a war-
ranty in regard of the same hogs and boar; of John de
Tudeham, son and heir of Edmund de Tudeham, of all his
land of la Clive with its appurtenances in the manor of
Staunton, and of common of all the waste lying between
the land of Robert de Selade and a spring below the
house of Philip and Richard de la Clive, a stream from
which runs to Blakeford, in turbaries, right of grazing,
&c., and of a rent of six pence yearly received from
a tenement of Roger de Sutton; of Henry de la Pome-
ray, of common of pasture in the manor of Vpotri;
of William de Say, son and heir of Robert son of
Reginald, of a virgate and half of land and of common
of pasture in the manor of Stanton, both for horses and
all other animals, &c.; of Hamelin de Baalun, of a

virgate and a half of land of waste in the same manor, with common of pasture there for thirty brood mares and three stallions and foals with their dams to the age of three years; of Ralph de Lestre, of one virgate of land in the manor of Bykehaulle, with two acres in Leggesheye and Middelheye; of Richard de Lestre, of the same lands; of Ralph de Lestre, of eleven shillings of annual rent, and of one pound and a half of wax for the lamp of the chapel of S. Mary of Tanton; of Master John de Chilewyke, of one messuage and one ferling of land at Bikehalle, with pasture for forty hogs free of feed, and common for all their beasts within and without the forest; of Richard de Lestre, of the land and common of pasture aforesaid; of Hugh de Pymor, son and heir of Robert de Slolegh, of one croft at Thurlasse; of Robert, son and heir of Jordan de Sloleghe, of land at Sloleghe with its appurtenances, and also of four acres north of Halfangre; of Robert de Munemue, of one dwelling-house in the vill of Brug-walter; of Cecilia de Monemuwe, of one dwelling-house in Brugeswalter with its appurtenances, liberties, and free customs; of Margaret de Monemuwe, daughter of Robert de Monemuwe, the acquittance of two dwelling-houses in the vill of Brugiswalter; of Henry de Bikebiric, chaplain, son of Cecilia la Bret, of land at Thurlakeston, and of four acres at Criche called Westmede; of Cecilia la Brette, lady and heiress of Thurlakeston and of Criche, of the lands aforesaid; of Johanna de Reigny, formerly wife of Thomas de Reigny, daughter and heiress of William de Bikebiric, the acquittance of her right in four acres called Westmede in Haneeriz; of Philip de Thurlakeston, son and heir of John de Thurlakeston, clerk, of all the land held aforetime by the said Philip in the manor of Thurlakeston; also, the acquittance of the said Philip, of all his rights in the said manor; of Geoffrey de Scoland, of an acre of land in the manor of Thurlakeston, together with the advowson of the church of the said manor; of Hugh de Wytheston, son of Robert, brother and heir of Ralph son of Robert, of a rent of one marc of silver from the land of Halswill; of Henry de Nuburgh, of the homage of John de Halswell and his heirs, and other services from the same land; of Gilbert de Thorne, of one ferling of land at Esse, and of one acre of meadow in Vinnedebere; of William de Thorne, son and heir of Gilbert, of a confirmation of the land aforesaid; of the same William, of the land called Bastardeswode, with one acre called Splottenewode; of the same William, of his land in Ryflet, within the lands already possessed by the Canons; of John de Thurlak, of half a virgate of land in Hoccomb; of the same John, of a meadow adjacent to one of Ralph Fitzwilliam; of Richard Thurlak, of five acres of land of the fee of Hoccombe; of Girard de Brocton, of land at Batpole; of Alina, daughter of Girard de Brocton, of one virgate of land with its appurtenances at Batpole in the manor of Muneketon; of William Fychet, son and heir of Hugh Fychet, a ratification of the aforesaid gift; of Richard de la Hide, son and heir of Ralph de la Hide, of land called Hesterlangedole; of Roger de Reigny, lord of Dulverton, an acquittance of a portion of the hundred of Dulverton; of Hawis de Pyn, formerly wife of Thomas de Pyn, an acquittance of all the portions of her hundred or court of Dulverton; of William de O., of the manor of Anestiges with all its appurtenances and liberties; of Richard de Weteden, to John then Prior of Taunton and his convent, of all his land of Dulverton, and of the rights therefrom acceding to him; of the same Richard, of all his land at Pleyston; of Emma, lady of Westowe, of all her land in Westowe; of Lucy Malet, daughter of Ralph

Fitzwilliam, a confirmation of the same; of Walter de Westowe, son and heir of Emma, an acquittance of all his right and claim in respect of the same land; of Thomas Cordary, son and heir of Ralph Cordary, of Bristoll, a confirmation of all the land of the said Thomas de Westowe; of Hugh de Nyweton, son and heir of Robert de Nyweton, a confirmation of all the land of the said Thomas; of Eva, formerly wife of Thomas le Cordery, of Bristoll, an acquittance of right and claim by dower in the land of Little Westowe called Modford; of Jordan de Molton, rector of the church of Lydyard S. Laurence, of all his land in Lydyard; of Gunnilda, widow of Adam Rys, of Taunton, of all the land of Lydyard S. Laurence; of the aforesaid Jordan de Molton, of the land of Pilclegh, with all its appurtenances; of Roger de Reigny, lord of Dulverton, of all his land of la Coumbe in the manor of Dulverton, with its appurtenances; of Richard de Turberville, of land which Humfrey the father of Hugh held, and also of the whole land of the moor of Hodiam; of Roger de Ho., son and heir of William de Ho., of all the land of the said Roger in Estdraydon and Westdraydon with all their appurtenances, and also of all his land of Hundcham, and of three ferlings in Aeswei, with their appurtenances; of Constance, formerly wife of John son of Theobald, of one ferling of land, one half next the land of the chapel of Hanetwill, and the other half in Curreslade, and of the produce of the wood which William the brother of the said Constance gave to her; of John, son of Theobald, of all his land in Curislade; of Adam de Childecote, of all the land which he held of the gift of William, lord of Childecote; of Luke de Punchardun, of the church of Cloneneburg, with its tithes and offerings, and other appurtenances, and of two ferlings of land, whereof each contains thirty acres, and of common of pasture of his land of Cloneneburg, pasturage of sheep and cattle, firewood, &c., by the testimony of his servant there; of William Punchardun, of the advowson of the said church of Cloneneburg; of Reginald, son and heir of Osbert of Bath, of two shillings to be received yearly from his manor of Radewille; of William Burcy, son and heir of William Burcy, of two shillings sterling yearly from his land of Ham; of Olivar Avenel, of the land of Hacche; of William Avenel, of the same; of Robert de Treberge, of all the land of Alwyneshill; of William Frauncleyn of Merigg, of one ferling of land with its appurtenances in Westowe, and of one messuage which Gregory Chanflur formerly occupied, and of two gardens in the same place; of Alina de Westowe, formerly wife of Richard Portbury, of a piece of land called Fotacre in Westornheye in Westowe, with all its appurtenances; of Richard Portbiry of Westowe, of four acres above la Westhill, of the old garden, with one acre which lies between that garden and the land of the aforesaid Prior; of the same Richard, of all his land in la Holmheye in the manor of Westowe; of William de Bremelhull, of thirteen acres and a half of land in Westowe; of Richard Portbury of Westowe, of all his land which he held in Westerfurshulle with its appurtenances in the manor of Westowe; of Richard Godwyne of Westowe, an acquittance of all right and claim in respect of a messuage, ten acres of arable, and half an acre of meadow land with their appurtenances in Westowe; of Jordan, son of Jordan de Hulle, of two shillings of annual rent from land which Henry de Lydyard, clerk, held, and of all the land which Elias de Hille held in Hille; of Maurice de Lege, of five acres of land in Esse; of William de Hulle, son and heir of Henry de Hulle, of all his arable land of Denebiri with its appur-

tenances, and of one acre of meadow in Donekesham; of
Jordan the son of Jordan de Hille, of land which Elias
de Hille held in Hille; of John de Hulle, son of Mericia
de Hulle, of two acres of land in Denebiric; of Jordan de
Harpeford, son and heir of David de Harpeford, of all the
land which Elias de Hille held in Hille; of William,
Bishop of Winchester, of all his land near Fons Saint
George in his manor of Tanton, with all the course of
the brook of Syreford near Tanton, for the grinding
of their corn, and all advantages thence to be derived.
The charter concludes with the usual form of concession
and confirmation of all the gifts enumerated. The witnesses are R[ichard de Bury]. Bp. of Durham, our Chan-
cellor; H[enry Burwash]. Bp. of Lincoln, our Treasurer;
John de Eltham, Earl of Cornwall, our dearest brother;
John de Warenne, Earl of Surrey; Henry de Percy;
William de Montcacute; Ralph de Neville, our Seneschal,
and others. It is dated at Westminster, the first day of
October.*

Here, as will be seen, are abstracts of upwards of one
hundred and thirty five documents, whereof a few only
have been noticed among the particulars which we have
already had before us, but our knowledge of the great
majority of which, and of the gifts which they conveyed,
is solely derived from this invaluable charter. Some of
them represent the grant of large possessions, and many
include the mention of several separate donations. The
first on the list alone records that of five churches with
their chapels and appurtenances. So numerous were the
endowments, and so rich the cartulary of Taunton Priory
in the year 1334.

On the 8th of November, 1334, the instrument of colla-

* Cart. 8 Edw. III., n. 12, mm. 5, 6. Appendix, No. XLVII.

tion of Walter de Burtone, S.T.P., Canon of Wells, to the subdeanery of that Cathedral Church, void by the death of Walter Broun, was dated at Tanton.*

On the 7th of December, 1334, Ralph the Prior, and Walter, prior of Brywton, were appointed by the Bishop collectors of the tenth voted to the king.†

In 1335, the Priory Church was still, as it appears, in need of funds for its completion, and a licence was granted to collect alms for that purpose for two years.‡

On the 17th of June, 1336, Geoffrey de Reyny was presented to the church of Combeflory, on the resignation of Tho. de Columbrugge.‖

The pious liberality of benefactors, great as it had hitherto been, was, however, not yet exhausted. The first Patent Roll of the 11th of Edward III. contains the particulars of the gift in fee farm by William de Montacute, earl of Salisbury, of the manor and hundred of Dulverton, with its appurtenances. The rent to be paid for this important concession was ten pounds a year. The witnesses to the instrument were Richard Lovel, John de Palton, John de Reigny, John de Menbury, Adam Le Brut, Ralph de Middelneye, Thomas de Orcharde, John atte Yerde, and others, names which, as in multitudes of other instances, the local reader will identify with those of places in the neighbourhood. It was dated in the Chapter House of the Priory of Taunton, on the 18th of March, 1337, and confirmed by the king at Westminster, on the 21st of the same month.§

---

* MS. Harl. 6966, p. 83. Appendix, No. XLVIII.
† MS. Harl. 6965, p. 84. Appendix, No. XLIX.
‡ MS. Harl. 6965, p. 101. Appendix, No. L.
‖ MS. Harl. 6965, p. 101. Appendix, No. LI.
§ Pat. 11 Edw. III. p. 1. m. 12. Appendix, No. LII.

The Conventual Church was still unfinished, though probably not much remained to be done. An Indulgence of fifteen days was granted, dated at Wyvelescomb, on the 10th of April, 1337, to all who should contribute towards its completion.* It was in this way that such stately fabrics were reared. The erection of our glorious mediæval Churches was the work not of a year or two, but of whole ages of faith, hope, and charity.

A difficulty here meets us which requires explanation.

We find, on the Close Roll of the 11th of Edward III., an instrument, dated at London, the 20th of November, 1337, and setting forth that Thomas, Prior of Bustlesham, and his Convent gave and confirmed to William de Montacute, earl of Salisbury, their founder, the manor of Hurdecote, and also ten marcs of annual rent which were paid by the Prior and Convent of Taunton on behalf of their manor and hundred of Dulverton, the grant of which has just been mentioned.† The gift to them, however, of these ten marcs does not appear in the earl's charter to the Priory of Taunton, in which nothing is said about any particular use to which the rent should be devoted. In the first Patent Roll of the 29th of Edward III., this difficulty is removed. It is there explained that the Prior and Convent of Taunton are to hold the manor and hundred of Dulverton, subject to the payment of an annual rent of ten pounds. Of this sum, as we shall see presently more in detail, they are to give ten marcs to the Prior and Convent of Bustlesham, and five marcs to the Custos of the chapel of Donyate. This is dated at Westminster, the 16th of April, 1355.

On the 22nd of March, 1338-9, Ralph de Colmpstoke

* MS. Harl. 6965, p. 110. Appendix, No. LIII.
† Claus. 11 Edw. III. p. 2. m. 13. Appendix, No. LIV.

resigned his office through the infirmities of extreme old age, and Robert de Messyngham was elected Prior in his stead, licence having been first obtained from Adam, Bishop of Winchester, the patron, on the 19th of the following April.* There were at the time of election twenty-five Canons belonging to the Priory, of whom twenty-four were present and one was abroad.†

On the 5th of November, 1339, Richard de Pym, chaplain, was presented by exchange to the vicarage of Kyngeston.‡ And a certain Walter, convicted of removing and injuring various crops, the property of William de Cammell, rector of Ivelton, was, on the 23rd of December, sentenced to do penance in several parish churches of the diocese, and that of Taunton among them.‖

On the 22nd of March, 1340, a writ was addressed to Ralph de Middelneye, the king's Eschaetor, to take the verdict of a jury relative to a third part of the Manor of Dulverton, proposed to be given to the Prior and Convent by Nicholas de Beleville. The course of procedure was exactly similar to that with which we are already acquainted. The verdict of the Jurors that the gift of such land would not be to the king's damage is dated at Lydyard S. Laurence, on the 12th of April; and the king's licence, for which the Prior paid a fine of five marcs, permitting the gift and receipt of the property was issued at Westminster on the 2nd of May.§

On the 6th of February, 1340-1, the Prior and Convent presented John Stede to the vicarage of Pipmynstr.¶

---

* MS. Harl. 6905, p. 127. Appendix, No. LV.
† Dr. Archer, from *Reg. Red.* 197. Appendix, No. LVI.
‡ MS. Harl. 6965, p. 130. Appendix, No. LVII.
‖ MS. Harl. 6965, p. 131. Appendix, No. LVIII.
§ Inquis. ad q. d. 14 Edw. III. (2. n.) n. 48. Pat. 14 Edw. III. p. 1. m. 2. 14 Edw. III. Rot. 24. Appendix, No. LIX.
¶ MS. Harl. 6905, p. 142. Appendix, No. LX.

In the same year, 1341, Taunton saw another monastic establishment attempted at least to be added to its ecclesiastical institutions. Little is known of this House, which was founded by Walter de Meryet, clerk, for monks of the order of Blessed Mary of Mount Carmel, or Whitefriars. As usual, we find a writ addressed to the king's Eschaetor, on the 28th of April, 1341, with the common enquiries, as already known to us, and the verdict, dated the Wednesday after Pentecost, or the 30th of May, 1341, at Taunton, of the Jurors summoned in accordance thereto. The present gift is one of nine acres of meadow land with their appurtenances in Taunton, which are said to be held by the said Walter of the Bishop of Winchester at a payment of seven shillings a year, and to be worth twenty shillings a year in all outgoings. The land is stated to be given for a certain Church and monastery which are to be there erected.[*] The king's licence in answer is dated at the Tower of London, the 14th of June.[†] There was evidently some difficulty in the way; and another writ was issued, dated the 12th of May, 1343, and an Inquisition taken at Bruggewater, before Edward de Stradlyng, the Eschaetor, relating to a property, probably the same, called Cokkesmede in Taunton. This Inquisition is dated on the Tuesday after the feast of SS. Peter and Paul, Apostles, which in the year 1343 was coincident with the 1st of July; and the Jurors were John de Membury, John Auger, John Punchardoun, John de Rodyngbere, Walter de Nythercote, Thomas atte Orcharde, John Snyffamor, Philip de Cloteworth, Richard atte Rysshyn, Thomas Mauncel, William de Haretrowe,

---

[*] Inquis. ad q. d. 15 Edw. III. (2 n.) n. 58. Appendix, No. LXI.
[†] Pat. 15 Edw. III. p. 2. m. 44. Appendix, No. LXII.

and Walter atte Withie. Although the verdict was favourable, the gift appears to have been over-ruled, and the proceedings ordered to be null and void.* This may account for the obscurity which envelopes the history of the House, and which a long search among the Records has not availed to dispel. Local tradition, which is always valuable, asserts that a Monastery was situated at a short distance westward from the Castle, in a place still called Paul's Field, near the Crescent; but it is probable that, if the Carmelite House were ever actually founded and occupied the site in question, it was but of short-lived duration, and that long before the general Dissolution in the sixteenth century it had ceased to exist. I may add that Walter de Meryet died on the 18th of May, 1345.

A licence for celebrating morning mass every day in the chapel of S. Mary Magdalene was granted on the 19th of March, 1341-2.†

It appears that Walter de Monyngton, one of the founders of Bathpool Mills, was confirmed Abbat of Glastonbury, at Taunton, on the 7th of November, 1342.‡

On the 29th of January, 1343-4, William de Aysshelcigh was presented to the vicarage of Kyngeston.∥

In 1346, Taunton had a new Prior. Robert de Messyngham died in the beginning of April; and Thomas Cok, a commission on the matter of whose confirmation was dated at Dogmersfeld on the 6th of that month,

---

* Inquis. ad q. d. 17 Edw. III. (2, n.) n. 43. Rott. Orig. 17 Edw. III. n. 13. Appendix, No. LXIII.
† MS. Harl. 6965, p. 149. Appendix, No. LXIV.
‡ MS. Harl. 6965, p. 153. Appendix, No. LXV.
∥ MS. Harl. 6965, p. 165. Appendix, No. LXVI.

was confirmed Prior in June.* Licence to elect had been granted at London on the 21st of March, the Convent's intimation of the election was dated in their Chapter House on the 30th of that month, and the Bishop of Winchester's assent to the same at Suthwerk on the 4th of April. A memorandum in the Register of William de Edyndon, Bishop of Winchester, further states that Brother Thomas le Couk, Prior of Taunton, on the 16th of June, in the presence of the venerable father William, Bishop of Winchester, in his manor of Suthwerk, did homage in person to the said father, as successor of the founder and patron of his House, by holding his joined hands between the hands of the said father, and saying, "I do you homage for the lands which I hold of you, and will bear you fealty against all people, saving the fealty to the king;" and that there were present at this homage lord Robert de Hungerford; Master John de Uske, Chancellor; and John de Beantre, Registrar.†

On the 4th of July, 1346, Robert Pippecote was presented to the Vicarage of Taunton, by exchange.‡

On the 18th of July, 1347, Thomas Floure was presented to Badyalton, by exchange; and on the 24th of November, Reginald Marchall to Thorlokkeston.‖

On the 1st of January, 1348-9, the same Reginald exchanged with Ralph Mareschal, who was admitted to Thurlokeston. William Wysman was presented to the Vicarage of Nyghenhyde, on the 11th of January; Hugh Lovegeer to the Vicarage of Dulverton, on the 11th of February; and William atte Stone to the vicarage of S. Mary Magdalene, on the 18th of the same month.§

* MS. Harl. 6965, p. 175. Dr. Archer, from Reg. Rad. 308. App. No. LXVII.
† E Reg. Will. de Edyndon, Wint. Ep. tom. I. ff. 8, 10b, 11. tom. II. fol. 8. Appendix, No. LXVIII.
‡ MS. Harl. 6965. p. 176. Appendix, No. LXIX.
‖ MS. Harl. 6965, pp. 186, 187. Appendix, No. LXX.
§ MS. Harl. 6965, pp. 195, 199, 202. Appendix, No. LXXI.

On the 22nd of March, William de Modbury was presented to the Church of Cumbeflory.*

On the 10th of April, 1349, John Cryspyn, chaplain, was presented to the Church of Rovyngton; and on the same day Robert Cox, chaplain, was presented to the vicarage of Pypminster.†

On the 25th of November, 1349, a solemn sentence was pronounced in the cemetery of the Conventual Church. After an investigation before John de Sydehale, Canon of Wells, the commissary specially appointed by the Bishop, Roger de Warmwille, of Ievele, was adjudged to do penance for various delinquencies of a very atrocious character. With bare head and feet he was thrice to make circuit of the church of Ievele, and during the celebration of high mass was to hold a wax candle of one pound weight, and at the conclusion of the penance to offer it at the high altar. The priest officiating was then to state to the clergy and people present the cause of the punishment. This was also to be done thrice in the public market, and in several churches of the diocese. He was in conclusion, after sundry scourgings, to pay to the Bishop twenty pounds sterling, as bail for future good behaviour, and to go on pilgrimage to the shrine of S. Thomas at Canterbury. Such was the mode in which the Church punished wealthy offenders in the fourteenth century—a mode personally to the culprit most distasteful, and thorougly appreciated by the community at large.‡

On the 22nd of June, 1350, the Prior and Convent presented John Cryspyn to Nihenhyde; and, on the same day, William Wysman to Rovyngton, and Richard Heryng to the vicarage of Putmynster, by exchange.¶

---

* MS. Harl. 0965, p. 205. Appendix, No. LXXII.
† MS. Harl. 6965, p. 207. Appendix, No. LXXIII.
‡ MS. Harl. 6965, pp. 211, 212. Appendix, No. LXXIV.
¶ MS. Harl. 0965, p. 212. Appendix, No. LXXV.

On the 18th of October, William Esch was presented to Nygenhuyde, on the resignation of John Cryspyn.*

On the 27th of January, 1350-1, Symon de Cherde was presented to the vicarage of Pypminstr.†

The year following witnessed a procedure very characteristic of the times. In order to enforce the performance of the essential duties of Christianity on every individual, the Church, recognizing alike her power and her responsibility towards those who were entrusted to her care, made it compulsory on all persons to attend their parish church, and to refrain from wandering to other churches to the consequent neglect of and absence from their own. Certain parishioners of Monkton rendered themselves liable to ecclesiastical censure on this account. It is probable that the distance at which they resided from their church had not a little to do with the matter. Portions of the parish of Monkton are but a few minutes' walk from the church of S. Mary Magdalene; while the parish church of Monkton lies at a distance of several miles, and the road, as we shall see by other evidences presently, was not in the very best condition. A mandate, however, bearing date the 21st of September, 1351, is directed by the Bishop to the vicar of Taunton, commanding him to check this presumption of the Monkton parishioners, by making strict search before the celebration of mass whether there were any from other parishes among the congregation, and, if so, to drive them from his church, and compel them to return to their own on pain of canonical censures.‡

On the 20th of October of the same year, Simon de Fareweye, parson of the church of Lidiard S. Laurence, had a writ of *Venire facias* issued against him to answer to

* MS. Harl. 6965, p. 230. Appendix, No. LXXVI.
† MS. Harl. 6965, p. 233. Appendix, No. LXXVII.
‡ MS. Harl. 6965, p. 239. Appendix, No. LXXVIII.

the Prior in the matter of his annual rent of two marcs, previously noticed in the Taxation of Pope Nicholas IV.*

It will be in the reader's recollection that in the Ordination of the vicarage of Taunton, in 1308, it was provided that the Prior should maintain at his own cost a curate to serve the chapels of Staplegrove and S. James's. In the year 1353 William atte Halle was curate. He complained to the Bishop that his proper stipend, tithes and offerings, were not paid, and that his bread and ale were not supplied as the law required. He therefore prayed for the Bishop's judgment in his favour. The Bishop did not, as it appears, entertain the curate's complaint. But William atte Halle was by no means to be overcome so easily, nor in any degree willing to resign his dues without a struggle for their preservation. Accordingly he forwarded an appeal to the Archbishop of the province, as right had been denied him nearer home; and the result was a mandate from the Primate to his brother at Wells, dated the 7th of June, 1353, requiring him either within fifteen days to see justice done to the said William, or to cite the Prior and Convent to appear in London before the Archbishop or his official at the church of S. Mary le Bow. The Bishop wisely took the latter course, and issued his citation, dated at Evercrich, the 21st of July, 1353, to Thomas Cocke the Prior and certain of his Canons to appear at the place and respond to the complaint aforesaid.† So little truth is there in the assumption that in these ages injustice could be done with impunity and without appeal. And, for aught that we know, the curate himself might have been in error, and his complaint without foundation.

In the October of the same year, R. C. a disobedient monk at Taunton—whether a member of the Priory is

* MS. Harl. 6965, p. 244. Appendix, No. LXXIX.
† MS. Harl. 6965, p. 265. Appendix, No. LXXX.

uncertain—was sent to the Priory of S. Germain's in Cornwall, for penance and imprisonment.*

On the 16th of April, 1355, the letters patent were issued to which allusion has already been made. They set forth that William earl of Salisbury, lately deceased, had given the manor and hundred of Dulverton, with all its appurtenances, by his indenture to the Prior and Convent of Taunton, to be held in fee farm by them and their successors, on their paying to the said earl and his heirs ten pounds a year. That the said earl had founded the monastery of Bustlesham, and had enriched it with sundry manors, lands, tenements and rents. That he had given to that monastery the sum of ten marcs out of the aforesaid ten pounds, and the remaining five marcs to the custos of the chapel of Donyate. And that the Prior of Taunton was to pay to each the ten and the five marcs respectively. That these moneys were to be used in aid of the said monastery of Bustlesham and chapel of Donyate, and for the performance of divine service daily in behalf of the king and the giver and their heirs. There had been some difficulty in the way of carrying out these provisions on the part of the Prior of Taunton, which on the petition of the Prior of Bustlesham was graciously removed, and both parties were empowered to proceed in agreement with the donor's intentions for their respective benefit.†

Matters in the Court of Exchequer, in Trinity Term, 1360, will be found detailed in a subsequent page.‡

In November, 1361, Prior Thomas de Pederton died, and on the 17th of January, 1361-2, the Canons received a new Prior in the person of Walter de Grateley. The licence to elect is dated at Suthwerke on the 23rd of

* MS. Harl. 6965, p. 258. Appendix, No. LXXXI.
† Pat. 29 Edw. III., p. 1. m. 6. Appendix, No. LXXXII.
‡ 34 Edw. III. Trin. Appendix, No. LXXXIII.

November, 1361; and the assent at the same place, 17th of January, 1361-2.*

On the 14th of February, 1361-2, William Wysman was presented to the church of Ronyngton.†

On the 10th of May, 1362, William de Essch was presented to the church of Thurlokeston, void by the death of Ralph Mareschal.‡

On the 17th of the same month, William Donekyn was presented to the vicarage of Nyhenhude, void by the resignation of William de Esse.|

On the 29th of December, 1377, Prior Walter de Grateley solemnly resigned his office in the Chapter House of the Conventual Church. He had long been suffering from the infirmities of age, and his House required a younger and more active head. There is a memorandum in the register of the famous William de Wykeham, Bishop of Winchester, which is of special interest as furnishing the names of the entire body of the Canons, fifteen in number, on this important though melancholy occasion. It is there stated that on the 29th day of December, 1377, the seventh year of the pontificate of Pope Gregory XI., there appeared, in the Chapter House of the Conventual Church of the Priory of SS. Peter and Paul, at Taunton, Master Thomas Spert, the official of John, Bishop of Bath and Wells, and specially deputed as his Commissary, Henry Persny and Walter Clopton, deputed by the Lord William, Bishop of Winchester, together with Thomas Duffeld, clerk, of the diocese of Sarum, notary public, in the presence of Brothers Walter Grateley, Prior, John Kyngesbury, sub-prior, Walter Cook, cellarer, Peter Ilmynstre,

---

* MS. Harl. 6961, p. 143. Rad. in Reg. Drok., 286. Reg. Edyndon, tom. 1. ff. 112b, 113b. Appendix, No. LXXXIV.
† MS. Harl. 6961, p. 144. Appendix, No. LXXXV.
‡ MS. Harl. 6961, p. 118. Appendix, No. LXXXVI.
| MS. Harl. 6961, p. 119. Appendix, No. LXXXVII.

sacristan, John Cley, precentor, Thomas Ilmynstre, Walter Gone, Thomas Grey, Roger Stacy, Thomas Askham, Tholomeus Frysel, John Welles alias Tappewere, John Tuleye, Robert Newton, John Croukorn, and John Russchton, Canons Regular of the said Conventual Church. Disputes had arisen about the observance of the rules, and it was also alleged that the administration of the House both in spirituals and temporals was partly neglected, owing to the said Prior being incapacitated by old age and other infirmities. Inquiries were made, and the Canons interrogated; and presently the said Prior submitted, and voluntarily tendered the resignation of his office to the said Commissary.*

The House appears to have been without a Prior for several months. It was not until the 18th of April, 1378, that William de Wykeham, Bishop of Winchester, patron of the Priory, granted to the Canons his licence to elect a Prior in the room of Br. Walter Gratcley their late Prior, the office being, as we have just observed, void by his free resignation and voluntary cession.† It appears that John de Kyngesbury, who in the already quoted list of dignitaries is named the sub-prior, was elected to the vacant office; for on the 1st of May, 1378, William de Wykeham, Bishop of Winchester, wrote from Suthwerk to John, Bishop of Bath and Wells, that he approved and consented to the election which had been made of Br. John de Kyngesbury to the Priorship of Taunton.‡

One of the most conspicuous and pleasing features of the landscape in the neighbourhood of the Priory was the lovely river that meandered through the fair vale of

* E Reg. Will. de Wykeham, Ep. Winton., vol. II., fol. clxvi. Appendix, No. LXXXVIII.
† Ibid., vol. II., fol. clxvi. Appendix, No. LXXXIX.
‡ Ibid. vol. II., fol. clxvi b. Appendix, No. CX.

Taunton in a thousand picturesque windings, as though loath to quit a scene of such rich and verdant beauty. Immediately at the foot of Creechbury Hill, at a distance of about a mile and a half from Taunton, were two well-known mills, called then, as now, Bathpool Mills, the property of the Abbats of Glastonbury, and rebuilt, if not originally founded, by Abbat Walter de Monyngton somewhere about the year 1364. The river furnished the motive power of these valuable establishments, and considerable jealousy was entertained of the use thus made of it and the advantage thus derived. The Patent Roll of the 8th of Richard II. contains a long and very interesting account of an Inquisition made at Taunton, on the Tuesday next after the festival of S. Egidius, in the sixth year of the aforesaid King, or the 2nd of September, 1382, to determine the truth of certain complaints made against the Abbat for various injuries done by these his mills, which, as it appears, he and his predecessors had held for eighteen years and upwards, to the river, its produce, and its trade. Among divers charges he is stated to allow willow and other trees to hang over the banks of the Tone in the parish of Monketon, so that boats are not able to pass as they were wont between the mill of Tobrigge and Bathepole. The site of Tobrigge mill was at some point of what is now called the Back Water,—with its sedgy pools fringed with old pollard willows, blackberry bushes, purple loosestrife, and hemp-agrimony—which was possibly the mill-leet, though, as I rather believe, the main channel of the stream, commencing at Firepool weir, at which perhaps the mill was situated, and rejoining the more modern though now ancient channel under a rustic bridge of wood at a short distance below Priory weir. It was also alleged that the mill for grinding corn called Bathepolemille projected from the bank of the river more by six feet than it did aforetime; that a fulling mill adjoining the said corn mill, erected by Richard de Acton after the great pestilence—that, perhaps, of 1369—and also in the hands of the aforesaid Abbat, was similarly objectionable; and that, by reason of these impediments to the water, the cornfields and pastures were inundated. The same injury and by the same means was alleged to be done to the king's highways between Taunton and Bathepolebrigge. This, the local reader will not fail to recollect, refers to the ancient highway, now for the most part disused, which runs for a considerable distance along the bank of the river above the mill, and is one of the most picturesque of the old Somersetshire roads, a very wilderness of verdure, the constant resort of gipsies who delight in its quiet and shady nooks, and well-known to and well-beloved by all Tauntonians. It was also asserted that, through the building of the mills, the boats which used to carry merchandise from Briggewater to Taunton could not go as formerly. The complainants seemed determined to make out a case, for they proceed to allege that the fish which used to swim from Briggewater to Taunton were so hindered by the aforesaid mills that they could no longer swim as they were wont. And they added that the bank of the river which used to be thirty feet in width, was then not more than ten or twelve feet at the most, from Bathepole as far as Cryche, so that boats could not pass as they used to do. The Abbat pleaded in reply to these charges that the trees complained of grew above the mill of Bathepole, where boats never went, nor ought to, nor could go; that the new buildings of the mills were exactly of the same depth, breadth, and height as the former had been; that there was a place in the lower part of the said mills, called Bathepolecrosse, up to which all boats came, time out of mind, from Briggewater towards Taunton, and

G

not higher nor further, but were there time out of mind discharged and unladen; that the Abbat had made a certain cist, through which the boats could be drawn in time of flood as far as the mill called Tobriggemill, and apart from this not above Bathepolecrosse; and that all injury arising from the impediments alleged to be caused by the willows and other trees was removed and entirely at an end. The Abbat thereupon obtained a verdict. The exemplification is dated, the King himself being witness, at Westminster, the 15th of December, 1384.*

Prior John de Kyngesbury was gathered to his fathers on the 5th of November, 1391. On the following day, Brother John Russchton, Sub-Prior, and the Convent of Taunton, wrote to William de Wykeham, Bishop of Winchester, to inform him that Br. John de Kyngesbury their Prior had departed this present life on the 5th of November, and that his body had been buried; and that, being without a Prior, they therefore begged that he their patron would grant them licence to elect another. The letter was dated in the Chapter House of their Conventual Church on the day aforesaid. On the 10th of November, the Bishop from his manor of Esshere granted to the Canons the licence which was thus solicited. On the 21st of the same month they proceeded to the election; and on that day Br. John Rysshton, Sub-Prior, and the Convent, wrote to the Bishop of Winchester informing him that they had elected Br. Walter Cook, one of their brothers and a Canon of their House, for their Prior, and prayed the Bishop's consent and approbation. This was given. On the 27th of November, William de Wykeham wrote from Esshere to Ralph, Bishop of Bath and Wells,

---

* Pat. 8 Ric. II., p. 2, mm. 43, 44. Appendix, No. XCI.

that he consented to the election that had been made of Br. Walter Cook as Prior of Taunton, and begged the Bishop to complete the said election.*

In 1397, the 21st of Richard II., the Prior is certified to have lent the King the sum of fifty marcs. At the same time the Abbats of Sherburn and Keynesham lent forty marcs each.†

In 1404, the famous William de Wykeham, Bishop of Winchester, bequeathed to the Prior and Convent one hundred marcs to pray for his soul. His will was dated the 24th of July, 1403, and proved the 9th of October, 1404.‡

On the 21st of June, in the 7th year of Henry IV, 1406, licence was given, on payment of twelve marcs, to Richard Otery, William Portman, Thomas parson of the Church of Munketon, and Thomas Scory, to give and assign to the Prior and Convent nine acres of meadow land with their appurtenances situate in Taunton; and to the said William to give one messuage with its appurtenances also in Taunton, after the death of Walter Knolle and Agnes his wife, who had a life interest in the property. The instrument concludes with the usual reservations, &c., and is dated at Westminster, the twenty-first day of June.‖

In the same year, Walter occurs as Prior. This was Walter Coke, who died in January, 1407-8.§

On the 18th of January, 1407-8, Robert Newton was elected, and on the 31st of the same month was confirmed Prior.¶

* E Reg. Will. de Wykeham, Ep. Winton., vol. 11., fol. ccli. App., No. XCII.
† Rymer, Fœd. Ed. Hag. tom. III., p. iv. 134. Appendix, No. XCIII.
‡ Appendix, No. XCIV.
‖ Pat. 7 Hen. IV., p. 2. m. 22. Appendix, No. XCV.
§ MS. Harl. 6966, p. 4. Dr. Archer, e Reg. Well. Apppendix, No. XCVI.
¶ MS. Harl. 6966, p. 4. Reg. Bowet, 48. Appendix, No. XCVII.

On the 20th of June, 1408, John Newman was presented to the Church of Ronyngton.*

On the 1st of June, 1409, occurs Robert, already noticed as Prior.†

On the 12th of August, 1413 (Collinson copied from Archer the erroneous date, 1431), Prior Robert Newton departed this life, and on the 1st of September Brother Thomas de Ufcolme, was elected Prior. He was confirmed in his office on the following day. There were then fourteen Canons in the House.‡

The injury alleged to be done to the trade of the river by the mills at Bathpool was again the subject of judicial investigation in the year 1414. An Inquisition was held at Taunton on the 5th of November, in that year, the 2nd of King Henry V. The Jurors, Thomas Osborn, Robert Grosse, Almaric atte Wythy, Robert Bullyng, William Snyffamor, Thomas Cachebar, John Haccombe, John Alrych, John Domet, Richard Fenbrygg, Matthew Short, and Robert Eysell, members of families which have already occurred in the course of this memoir, affirmed that a certain Walter, the immediate predecessor of the then Abbat of Glastonbury, had made a certain watercourse adjoining the said Bathepolemylle so narrow with an obstruction of timber and massive masonry, through the midst of the channel of the river between Taunton and Bryggewater, that the river craft — "vocat' Botes et Trowys"—with their various freight, to wit, firewood, timber, charcoal, pitch, salt, iron, lime, grain, ale, wine, &c., rather a goodly list of Taunton requirements in the fourteenth and fifteenth centuries, could not reach

* MS. Harl. 6066, p. 14. Appendix, No. XCVIII.
† MS. Harl. 6066, p. 5. Appendix, No. XCIX.
‡ MS. Harl. 6066, p. 30. Dr. Archer, e Reg. Well. Appendix, No. C.

their destination by reason of these his enclosures and impediments, to the loss and damage of a thousand pounds and much more, if a remedy were not quickly applied.*

On the 18th of November, 1415, Prior Thomas Ufcolme was summoned to Convocation at S. Paul's in London. Among others similarly summoned were John, Prior of Bath; Walter Medford, Dean of Wells; John, Abbat of Glastonbury; John, Abbat of Muchelney; Leonard, Abbat of Clyve; John, Abbat of Athelney; and John, Prior of Bruton.†

In 1415 Orders were celebrated in the Church of S. Mary Magdalene.‡

On the 14th of January, in the 5th of Henry VI., 1426-7, an Inquisition was taken with respect to a chantry founded in the Church of S. Mary Magdalene by Robert de Bathe and Tiffina his wife, who demised four messuages with their appurtenances in Taunton, in the occupation of John Walshe, Philip Gent, Walter Hulling, and Alice Lytell, respectively, of the value of twenty-six shillings and eight pence a year, for the use of the fraternity of the Holy Cross in the aforesaid Church, to provide a priest for such chantry. The bequest was originally made on the 10th of December, 1397, and now took effect on the deaths of the donors. The King's licence is dated at Westminster, the 13th of May, 1427.||

On the 5th of October, 1429, Thomas occurs Prior as presenting to Clannaborough.§

* Inquis. ad q. d. 2 Hen. V., n. 13. Appendix, No. CI.
† MS. Harl. 6966, p. 21. Appendix, No. CII.
‡ MS. Harl. 6965, p. 31. Appendix, No. CIII.
|| Inquis. p. m. 5 Hen. VI., n. 62. Appendix, No. CIV.
§ Dr. Oliver, from Reg. Exon. Appendix, No. CV.

In 1437 John Warr founded and endowed a chapel of S. Mary Magdalene, in the Church of S. Margaret, at Taunton, already mentioned in this memoir, for one or two chaplains.*

Time, which brings mutation to all things, is now about to carry us into days of commotion, disorder and trouble. Among other evidences of violated peace, several councils were convened for the purpose of introducing alterations into the ecclesiastical system at large, in which the judgment of the Christian world was exercised in the vain attempt of satisfying the ever-craving desires of men who are given to change, and love things more or less in proportion to their novelty. One of these councils was held at Ferrara, in order to bring about a favourite design of many, the union of the Greek and Latin Churches. Thomas Benet, Prior of Taunton, was summoned to this council in April, 1438.†

In the year 1444 the revenues of the Priory were valued at £146 13s. 4d.‡

Some unpleasantness occurred about this time in connexion with the chapel of Wilton. It will be remembered that Fons S. George was one of the chapels annexed to the vicarage of S. Mary Magdalene, and that the vicar was to serve the same at his own proper cost by himself or his curates. This he appears to have omitted to do, and a summons was issued on the 29th of March, 1444, to enquire into the reasons of his neglect.‖

Orders were celebrated in the Church of S. Mary Mag-

---

* MS. Harl. 6966, p. 48. Appendix, No. CVI.
† MS. Harl. 6966, pp. 49, 50. Reg. Staff. 145. Appendix, No. CVII.
‡ Dr. Archer, a Reg. Well. Appendix, No. CVIII.
‖ MS. Harl. 6966, p. 58. Appendix, No. CIX.

dalene, on the 19th of September, by the Bishop of Bath
and Wells. Robert Stillyngton, LL.D. of the diocese of
York, was ordained acolite and sub-deacon.*

The Bishop appears to have prosecuted enquiries, similar
to those just detailed, in respect of the other vicars and
curates. On the 21st of September, in the same year,
several of these, among whom was Richard Pomerey, chaplain of the chantry of S. Andrew in the Church of S. Mary
Magdalene, were admonished under pain of excommunica-
tion to be more observant for the future of the customs and
duties of their cures.†

Richard Glene, Prior, occurs on the 12th of June, 1449,
and was summoned to Convocation in the same year.‡

In 1452 it appears that the Priory was burdened above
measure by the delivery of bread and ale to various reci-
pients in Taunton both of the poor and of the servants of
the House. Large as were the means at command, the
doles had become excessive. The Bishop issued his mandate, dated the 28th of November, as to how far such
doles should be stayed, and that the serving men of the
said monastery should be paid according to their labours
in eatables, and drinkables, and convenient salaries, as
agreement could better be made with the same.‖ .

John Valens, chaplain, was presented to the Church of
Lydyard S. Laurence, and bound by oath to pay an annual
pension of ten marcs to his predecessor Thomas Drayton,
resigning on account of old age and infirmity.§ It is
possible that this may not be the exact place which this

* MS. Harl. 6966, p. 120. Appendix, No. CX.
† MS. Harl. 6966, p. 58. Appendix, No. CXI.
‡ MS. Harl. 6966, p. 67. Reg. Bek. 89. Appendix, No. CXII.
‖ MS. Harl. 6966, p. 74. Appendix, No. CXIII.
§ MS. Harl. 6966, p. 107. Appendix, No. CXIV.

notice should occupy in chronological order; but I have no means of rectifying the error, if such it be.

At an Ordination held in the Church of S. Mary Magdalene, on the 8th of March, 1459-60, John Arnold, M.A., of New College, Oxford, was ordained deacon, and priest on the 29th of the same month.*

An Inquisition held in the Chapel of S. Martin, at Bowe, on the 6th of August, 1470, found that the right of patronage of S. Petrock's, Clannaborough, in the Deanery of Chumleigh, was vested in the Prior and Convent of Taunton, and that they received four shillings per annum, on account of a certain glebe of some fifty acres.†

On the 24th of October, 1470, Richard (Glene), Prior, and his Convent, give the first presentation of the Church of Lydiard S. Laurence to Robert Stowell, John Cheyne, and John Trevilian.‡

A Hospital for lepers had been founded near the Chapel of S. Margaret, as early as or before the year 1280, the advowson of which was then given to the Abbat and Convent of Glastonbury by Thomas Lambryth.‖ The charity was at this time in need of pecuniary assistance, and on the 8th of July, 1472, William Wayneflete, Bishop of Winchester, by an instrument dated at Suthwerke as aforesaid, granted an Indulgence of forty days to all who should extend helping hands and contribute of their goods to the pious work. The Indulgence was to last for a period of five years.§

---

* MS. Harl. 6066, p. 123. Appendix, No. CXV.
† Dr. Oliver, from Reg. Both., fol. 67. Reg. Fox, f. 148. Appendix, No. CXVI.
‡ MS. Harl. 6966, p. 130. Appendix, No. CXVII.
‖ Cart. Glaston. MS. Macro., fol. 119b. Appendix, No. CXVIII.
§ E Reg. Dnl. Will. Wayneflete, Ep. Winton. tom. 11., fol. 152. Appendix, No. CXIX.

Richard Glene, Prior, died on the 31st of January, 1475-6.*

On the 1st of February, 1375-6, the Sub-prior and Convent addressed a letter from their Chapter House and under their common seal to William Wayneflete, Bishop of Winchester, informing him of the death of their Prior, Richard Glene, on the previous day, and soliciting him for licence to elect another. The Bishop issued his licence, dated the 9th of February, from his house in the parish of S. Olave, Suthwerk. On the 23rd of the same month, the Sub-prior and Convent, fifteen in number, addressed another letter from their Chapter House and under their common seal to the Bishop, setting forth that, out of the superlative confidence which they had in his government, they had unanimously elected him their arbiter, and supplicating him to take this burden upon him, and to choose from among their community as their future Prior one who should be devout towards God, faithful to his patron, useful to the House, and, as they hoped, affectionate to his brethren and mindful of their interests. By an instrument given under his seal in his manor of Waltham, on the 27th of February, Bishop Wayneflete acknowledged the receipt of this letter, and in virtue thereof nominated John Asshe, a Canon of their Priory and one of their brethren, of the Order of S. Augustine, and in the said Priory expressly professed, of the lawful age, and in Priest's Orders, &c., to the office of Prior, and to govern the said Priory. The Sub-prior and Convent being informed of this, accepted the said John Asshe, and, by an instrument under their common seal and dated in their Chapter House at Taunton, certified that they had elected John Exeeter, a Canon

---

* MS. Harl. 6066, p. 144. Appendix, No. CXX.

and brother of their House, to be their procurator, for the purpose of presenting the elect to the Bishop, and to obtain his assent and all other things belonging to his office of patron. Finally, by a document dated in his manor at Waltham, on the 17th of March, Bp. Wayneflete informs the Sub-prior and Convent that he had received their procurator, John Exeeter, and that the Prior elect had been presented to him; and that by these presents he gave his consent and assent to the said elect and election.*

John Prowse occurs as Prior in 1492.†

On the 3rd of September in the same year, Thomas Birde, one of the Canons of the House, was elected Prior of Berlich, and confirmed on the 6th of that month.‡

John Prowse occurs also in 1497.∥

Two years afterwards saw the Prior of Taunton admitted to one of the most covetted honours that the Church could bestow. By a bull, dated at Rome the 4th of May, 1499, Pope Alexander VI. conceded to his beloved son John and his successors, the privilege of using the ring, pastoral staff, and other pontifical ornaments save the mitre; also of pronouncing solemn benediction after mass, vespers, compline, &c., when, however, at such benediction there should be present no bishop nor legate of the Apostolic see; and of admitting to Minor Orders the Canons and choristers of the said monastery.§ This, we may be sure, was welcomed as one of the crowning acquisitions of the noble House to which it was conceded. The original

---

* MS. Harl. 6966, p. 144. Reg. Well. Stillington. Reg. Dni. Will. Wayneflete, Ep. Winton. vol. II. ff. 37b—39b. Appendix, No. CXXI.

† Dr. Archer, from Reg. Fox. Appendix, No. CXXII.

‡ MS. Harl. 6966, p. 149. Appendix, No. CXXIII.

∥ MS. Harl. 6966, p. 153. Appendix, No. CXXIV.

§ MS. Harl. 6966, p. 153. Appendix, No. CXXV.

instrument is still to be found among the MSS. at Lambeth, and from it I have copied all that is now legible.* Many words have entirely perished from the combined influence of neglect and damp, and a single touch would be sufficient to remove many more. It commences with praise of the sincere devotion and religious excellence of the community, and grounds upon these reasons the honors and concessions which follow, removing from them and each of them all ecclesiastical sentences, censures, and punishments, and proceeding to confer on the Prior and his successors the favours which have been already enumerated. The document is of special interest not only to the historian of Taunton Priory, but to the student of monastic annals in general. For although it was not uncommon to grant to the Heads of the more important Religious Houses the privilege of using the Paramenta Pontificalia, which consisted, as we learn from the Ritualists, of sandals, amice, albe, girdle, pectoral cross, stole, tunic, dalmatic, gloves, mitre, ring, staff, and maniple, and of giving Episcopal Benediction in the Church and Refectory, it is the only instance with which I am acquainted, and I am not alone in this particular, of a Prior being authorised to promote to Minor Orders the inmates of his own community. This, however, is distinctly stated—"Canonicos quoq' et chorales dicti monasterii ad minores ordines promouere libere ac licite unleatis."

Another bull accompanied this in favour of the Priory. The document follows the one just quoted in the volume wherein it and many others have some ages ago been together though loosely mounted. Unhappily it is in even worse condition than its predecessor, while both of

* MSS. Lambeth. No. 643, art. 13. Appendix, No. CXXVI.

them are among the most frayed and effaced in the whole collection, and is scarcely intelligible from the number of words either obliterated in the body of the MS. or torn away from the edge.* It appears to have been in defence of the Priory against certain "injuriatores," and in confirmation of the antecedent bull. It is addressed to the Bishops of Worcester and Exeter, and, as it seems, although the mutilations render this not quite certain, to the Abbat of Glastonbury, approving and confirming certain privileges, enjoining them to see to the solemn publication and effectual reception of the aforesaid letters, and concluding with a reference to the secular arm, in case, it may be presumed, of any disobedience or opposition on the part of the enemies of the House. The date of both instruments is apparently the same—the 4th of May, 1499. A very interesting addition to each is the endorsement, "vij° Augsti a° 1537. Taunton." written in a hand corresponding in age with the period recorded, and furnishing us, as we shall see presently, with the date of a circumstance which was hitherto unknown.

On the 17th of December, 1501, John Samson, priest, was presented to the vicarage of Nynhede, on the resignation of John Prowse, the Prior.†

On the 16th of September, 1502, John Prowse, Prior, was presented to the Church of Lydeyard S. Laurence, on the decease of John Vowell, by Nicholas Dissham, to whom the right of presentation had been conceded for that turn by the Prior and Convent.‡

On the 20th of September, in the same year, John

---

* MSS. Lambeth, No. 612, art. 14. Appendix, No. CXXVII.
† MS. Harl. 6966, p. 161. Appendix, No. CXXVIII.
‡ MS. Harl. 6966, p. 165. Appendix, No. CXXIX.

Baker, chaplain, was presented to the Church of Comflory, on the resignation of John Prows, Prior of Taunton.*

On the 29th of June, 1504, a faculty of plurality was granted to Hugh Thomas, vicar of S. Mary Magdalene; and on the 29th of the following October, he was presented to the vicarage of Dulverton, on the resignation of John Edyngton: the said John to receive an annual pension of £6 13s. 4d.†

On the 11th of September, 1505, Thomas Symons was presented to the Church of Thurlockston, on the resignation of John Symmys: to pay the said John an annual pension of 6s. 8d.‡

Once more we have an account of various complaints which were made of the injury done by certain mills to the neighbouring lands. On this occasion it was the mill of Northcory which was the cause of offence, as inundating and injuring the meadows. In the Wells Register is a letter from the Chapter to the Bishop of Winchester in extenuation of the alleged grievance, dated October, 1505.‖

John Trygge was presented to the vicarage of Nynehede on the 9th of September, 1507, on the resignation of John Sampson: to pay to the said John an annual pension of 40s.§

On the 30th of October, 1508, William Bury, M.A., succeeded Hugh Thomas, deceased, in the vicarage of S. Mary Magdalene, on the presentation of John Prows, Prior, and Convent.¶

* MS. Harl. 6966, p. 165. Appendix, No. CXXX.
† MS. Harl. 6967, f. 3. Appendix, No. CXXXI.
‡ MS. Harl. 6967, f. 4b. Appendix, No. CXXXII.
‖ MS. Harl. 6968, p. 45. Appendix, No. CXXXIII.
§ MS. Harl. 6967, f. 8. Appendix, No. CXXXIV.
¶ MS. Harl. 6967, f. 10. Appendix, No. CXXXV.

On the 4th of November, in the same year, Thomas Cokysden was presented by the same John Prows, Prior, and Convent, to Nynehead, on the resignation of John Trigge: to pay to the said John Trigge an annual pension of 40s.*

On the 29th of November, in the same year, Peter Druet, M.A., was presented by the same John and his Convent to the vicarage of Dulverton, void by the death of Hugh Thomas. He was to continue the payment of the annual pension of £6 13s. 4d. to the former vicar, John Edyngton, who, after the manner of annuitants, still survived.†

On the 2nd of April, 1509, William Mors, LL.D., was presented to the vicarage of Pytmyster by the same John and Convent, on the death of Richard Mader. William Mors had obtained a dispensation for plurality, and that the Churches of S. Mary of Corscombe and of S. Dubricius of Porloke should be united to his prebend of Combe Secunda, on his assertion that the income of those two Churches did not exceed £26 13s. 4d. per annum.‡

John Prows was summoned to convocation, in December, 1509. Among others summoned at the same time were Richard Beer, Abbat of Glastonbury; Thomas Broke, Abbat of Mochilney; John Wellyngton, Abbat of Athelney; and John Peynter, Abbat of Clyve.‖

On the 11th of August, 1511, Richard Pleysse was presented to the vicarage of Kyngyston, on the death of Robert Good.§

---

* MS. Harl. 6967, f. 10. Appendix, No. CXXXVI.
† MS. Harl. 6967, f. 10. Appendix, No. CXXXVII.
‡ MS. Harl. 6967, f. 11. Appendix, No. CXXXVIII.
‖ MS. Harl. 6967, f. 12b. Appendix, No. CXXXIX.
§ MS. Harl. 6967, f. 15. Appendix, No. CXL.

John Prows, Prior, resigned his dignity on the 3rd of February, 1513-4.

On the day just mentioned the Sub-prior and Convent made humble supplication to Richard, Bishop of Winchester, for licence to elect another Prior, representing that their late head, John Prous, had freely resigned his dignity, and that the House so deprived was widowed and destitute of the comfort of a Prior and pastor. To avoid the injury that from this state of things would ensue, they solicit his licence to proceed to the election. The letter was dated in their Chapter House on the 3rd day of February, 1513. On the 11th of the same month the licence was granted. The Bishop enjoins them to choose for their Prior and pastor a man devoted to God and apt in all things for the government of the House, one able to defend and protect its rights in all things, and faithful and obedient to himself his ecclesiastical superior and patron.*

Their choice fell upon Nicholas Peper. He was elected on the 23rd of February, 1513-4, thirteen Canons being present and three absent. We find him in the same year summoned to convocation, together with the Abbats of Glastonbury, Mochelney, and Athelney, just mentioned, and William Dovele, Abbat of Clyve.†

On the 1st of September, 1514, John Hyll, bachelor of law, was presented to the Church of Combeflory, on the resignation of John Baker: an annual pension of five marcs to be paid to the said John Baker.‡

In November, 1515, Nicholas Peper was again summoned to convocation.‖

---

* E Reg. Dni Ric. Fox, Winton. Ep. tom. III. fol. 30. Appendix, No. CXLI.
† MS. Harl. 6967, ff. 19b, 24b. Dr. Archer, from Reg. Adrian. Appendix, No. CXLII.
‡ MS. Harl. 6967, f. 20. Appendix, No. CXLIII.
‖ MS. Harl. 6967, f. 21. Appendix, No. CXLIV.

John Prows, formerly Prior, died in the earlier part of 1519, and John North succeeded him on the 11th of May in that year in his benefice of Lediard S. Laurence.*

On the 17th of February, 1519-20, Thomas Wyse, bachelor of law, succeeded William Mors, deceased, in the vicarage of Pytminster, on the presentation of John Tregonwyl, clerk, patron for that turn by the concession of the Prior and Convent.†

Robert Morwent, M.A., succeeded John North, deceased, in the Church of Ledyard S. Laurence, on the 9th of August, 1521.‡

On the 10th of April, 1522, Robert Huet was presented to the Church of Rovington, on the death of Robert Tedworth.‖

On the 12th of August, 1523, John Hogans was presented to the church of Thorlakyston, on the death of Thomas Symons, by Nicholas, Prior of Taunton, and Convent.§

Nicholas Peper, Prior, died on the 26th of September, 1523; and on the 19th of November following, William Yorke, Canon of Bruton, was nominated Prior by Cardinal Wolsey, to whom the House had given licence to appoint a successor. There were on this occasion twelve Canons present, and one absent.¶

On the 2nd of December, 1524, John Slocock was presented to the vicarage of Dulverton, on the resignation of William Bowreman.**

---

* MS. Harl. 6967, f. 26. Appendix, No. CXLV.
† MS. Harl. 6967, f. 27b. Appendix, No. CXLVI.
‡ MS. Harl. 6967, f. 29b. Appendix, No. CXLVII.
‖ MS. Harl. 6967, f. 30b. Appendix, No. CXLVIII.
§ MS. Harl. 6967, f. 42b. Appendix, No. CXLIX.
¶ MS. Harl. 6967, f. 47b. Dr. Arober, e Reg. Clerk. Appendix, No. CL.
** MS. Harl. 6967, f. 43b. Appendix, No. CLI.

On the 21st of April, 1526, John Hill was presented to the Church of Runyngton, on the death of Robert Huet.*

William Wyneyard, M.A., succeeded, on the 13th of March, 1526-7, to the vicarage of Pytmynster, vacant by the resignation of James Henton.†

On the 21st of March, 1529-30, James Dowdyng was presented to the Church of S. Egidius of Thurlokeston, on the resignation of John Ogans.‡

We have now arrived at the period of a transaction which availed to make yet another accession to the power and wealth of the Priory. The history of the proceeding has hitherto been very obscure, but sufficient can be presented to render it intelligible. There was a small and little known Priory, dedicated to S. James, and founded for Canons of the order of S. Augustine and the regulation of S. Victor, at Staffordell or Staverdale, about three miles from Wincanton. The Priory Church was the mother church of the neighbouring town. The honour of the foundation is divided between Sir William Zouche and Richard Lovel, lord of the Manor of Wincanton, to each of whom it is attributed. The former seems to have been the actual founder, but the latter so considerable a benefactor as to merit an almost equal share of praise for the good work. The Priory was endowed with lands in Wincanton, Prestley, Rackington, Eastrepe, Cattlesham, Thorn-Coffin, and other places in the county of Somerset, and in Buckham-Weston, in the county of Dorset. In the 24th of Edward III., Sir Richard Lovel, knt., founded a chantry in the Priory Church, with a messuage, a mill, two carucates of arable land, twelve acres of meadow,

* MS. Harl. 6967, f. 37b. Appendix, No. CLII.
† MS. Harl. 6967, f. 38b. Appendix, No. CLIII.
‡ MS. Harl. 6967, f. 33b. Appendix, No. CLIV.

twelve acres of pasture, ten acres of wood, and the rent
of one pound of pepper, with their appurtenances situated
in Presteleye, for a Chaplain to say daily service for the
souls of himself, his father, mother, ancestors, and all the
faithful departed. The Inquisition was dated at Bruton,
on the 12th of October in the year aforesaid.[*] Many
members of the families of S. Maur and Zouch found a
last resting place in the Conventual Church, which, having
become ruinous, was rebuilt by Sir John Stourton, knt.,
and consecrated on the 4th of June, 1443. The names of
a few of the Priors have been recovered, and I hope at a
future period to add from our MSS. repositories some
additions which I possess to our present amount of pub-
lished information. I am now only concerned with the
House from its annexation to Taunton, which came about
in the following manner.

William Grendon, Canon of Taunton, was elected Prior
of Staverdale in 1524. Not long after his election he
appears to have taken steps to unite his Monastery to his
former and we may imagine favourite home. In this
attempt he succeeded, and, with consent of his Convent,
the union was effected in the 24th year of Henry VIII.
The king's licence for this proceeding is entered on the
Patent Roll of that year, and conveys permission to
William Grendon, Prior of Staffordell, or Staverdale, to
give and concede the whole of their possessions, and rights
belonging thereunto, including the site, circuit, and precinct of the Priory itself, together with all and singular its
churches, chapels, cemeteries, sanctuaries, manors, lord-
ships, messuages, houses, mills, dovecots, gardens, lands,
tenements, reversions, rents, services, court leets, views of

---

[*] Inquis. p. m. 24 Edw. III. (2 n.) n. 10.

franc-pledge, advowsons of churches, chapels and chantries, marshes, waters, fisheries, vivaries, warrens, and all other inheritances whatsoever, to William Yorke, Prior of Taunton, and his Convent for ever. And further, of his more abundant grace, the king gives the advowson, although held of himself in capite, of the Parish Church of Wyncalnton, hitherto enjoyed by the Prior and Convent of Staverdale, to the Prior and Convent of Taunton, without fine or fee great or small. The Patent is dated, witness the king himself, at Westminster, the 9th of April, 1533.*

At this point we may conveniently stay our progress, and endeavour to realize the more striking features of that pleasant picture of cloister life and mediæval usage which the varied details before us, culled from all sources and directions, may easily present to our intellectual vision. First in the foreground stands a noble establishment, the home of all the religion, learning, and civilization of the age, the fount and centre of that gracious influence which alone rescued England for many generations from moral degradation and mental barbarism. Here was located a sacred community that gave, so far as such was possible, a tone of refinement to the neighbourhood which its presence ennobled, the patrons and supporters of everything that could dignify, elevate, and adorn mankind. In this and similar places, green islands of devotion in the midst of the world's desert, calm houses of escape from unruly violence and the strife of tongues, quiet abodes of thoughtful meditation and saintly counsel, religion found a home specially suited to her holy mind. Sacred literature but for them would have left the world, and art but for them would have had no

* Pat. 24 Hen. VIII., p. 2, m. (31)5. Appendix, No. CLV.

students. Most that we now enjoy and value is their precious and sacred bequest. The remains which we possess of ancient learning, whether sacred or secular, the consequent knowledge of our divine religion, the very bells that still call us to prayer, and the churches that usually receive men who respond to the invitation, our libraries, our colleges, our schools, our hospitals, all tell of those old ages of faith and patience, and make forgetfulness of their graces an ingratitude and a sin. It is nothing to the purpose that some of their enemies have taken delight in exposing the rare instances where the cloister concealed practices against which morality protests. It would indeed be strange, if, among the multitude of Religious Houses which then covered the face of England, some few deviations from rectitude were not to be discovered. As long as human nature continues to be what it is, so long it would be madness and folly to expect any other result. This, however, must by no means be allowed to prejudice the case of the great majority of such establishments. The evils that were found in a few of them—and the greatest wonder is that the instances were not more numerous—were, and still are, prominently displayed, and execration of them is sedulously courted; while the immaculate condition of the general body, a fact admitted even by unscrupulous enemies who had an interest in proving them as degraded as possible, is too often passed over, even by those who ought to know better, as a matter of no importance and unworthy of remark. Such persons are contenders not for truth but for party.

The external garb of the bountiful and gracious monastic spirit was no doubt magnificently represented in Taunton Priory. For many generations the Augustine Canon was celebrated as uniting in his single person the accordant

excellencies of the scholar and the saint. He was both
patron and professor of the literature of his age; and his
home breathed of the refinement of his elegant mind, and
bore the impress of his exquisite taste. Here the master
influence was most conspicuously evidenced. Here, in their
beautiful House, amid sights and sounds that fit men for
heaven, amid holy labours and the quiet study of earlier
Christianity, lived, as I have elsewhere endeavoured to
picture them and their brethren, the inmates of the fair
Priory of Taunton. Removed from the petty cares of
ordinary existence, they attained to a degree of mental
cultivation to which few others could aspire. And this
was combined in numberless instances with that clear and
sagacious perception of the character of their times, which
made them accomplished men of society as well as profound
students of the cloister. A body of ecclesiastics thus ruled
for several centuries the religious destinies and spiritual
life of Taunton; and their government, so far as we can
now arrive at an insight into it, was characterized by the
excellencies of the rulers themselves. The outer man, too,
symbolized the inner, for even in the Canon's very aspect
there was that which was imposing in no little degree.
He wore an albe that reached to the foot, and was fastened
round the waist with a girdle of black leather. His amice
enwrapped his shoulders like a cloke. Over these he had
a long black mantle, to which was fastened a hood of the
same colour; and a high black cap covered his head, and
contrasted well with his flowing beard. Few ecclesiastics
of other Orders could have rivalled either in mental
dignity or in external bearing the Augustine Canon of
Taunton.

The Church and Priory were no doubt worthy of the
companionship. That the former was magnificent we have

positive proof. We can catch but a glimpse, however, of its beauties, and with that must endeavour to be content. As we have already seen, it was commenced as early as, if not previous to, the year 1277, and was still unfinished in 1337. It will thus be apparent to the architectural reader that the edifice was erected in the best and purest age of constructive art. The "Early English" was passing into the "Decorated" at the beginning of the interval, and before its close the latter style had arrived at its full exuberance of beauty. Of the other peculiarities of the structure, although we may be sure that it harmonised in its perfection with the charming scene which lay around it, we are unhappily possessed of no memorial. The only guess that we can make with any degree of probability, is that it had an ornament to which the builders both of the Early English and Decorated periods were greatly indebted for the marvellous effect of the exteriors of their edifices—a lofty spire at the junction of the transept with the nave and choir. Thus much the Common Seal of the Priory would suggest, in which one of the two Apostles to whom the House was dedicated is represented holding such a church in his right hand. The domestic portion of the Priory, too, was certain to be a collection of goodly edifices. Mention has already been made of the Chapter House; but of quiet cloister and lordly refectory, scriptorium, guest-house, infirmary, and dormitory, the record is gone, we fear, for ever. And yet all were assuredly splendid of their kind, as the home of a community wealthy and powerful, and the frequent resort of the noble and renowned. The Lord Prior and his Canons often found themselves surrounded by personages of public importance in Church and State; and their lodging and cheer were doubtless agreeable to their condition, and indicative of that spirit of liberal

The Site of Taunton Priory.

Dunkeswell Priory. Bath. Dunkeswell.

hospitality which the rule alike of Religion and of their Order did so much to foster.

There can be little doubt that the great entrance gateway of the Monastery was in Canon Street, so called after the dignitaries of the House, and in which the massive foundations of ancient edifices, not improbably belonging to them, have repeatedly been discovered. How far the buildings extended towards the east and south we have no means of knowing, save by the indications already referred to. There is, however, on the left hand of the visitor as he enters the fields, a large and picturesque barn, containing some work of the sixteenth century, but in which have been inserted by the questionable dictate of modern taste, several ornamental details of uncertain derivation. [*See the Plates.*] This may be taken as the limit of the Conventual buildings in the northern direction.

Notwithstanding the silence of historians and the absence of manuscript authority on the subject, it is next to certain that the Conventual Church, like multitudes of similar structures, was a favourite place of sepulture. The only asserted instance which I have met with is unfortunately founded on error. It is that of Jasper Tudor, duke of Bedford and earl of Pembroke, the half brother of King Henry VI., who died in 1497, and, by his will, dated the 15th of December, 1495, is said to have ordered his body to be interred in this monastery, and also that a monument should be erected over it, and that forty pounds a year should be paid out of his lands for four priests to pray for ever for the health of his soul, and for the souls of his father, of Katharine, sometime Queen of England, his mother, of Edmund, earl of Richmond, his brother, and of all other his predecessors.[*] It was Keynsham, however, and not Taunton, which was thus selected.

[*] Dugd. Bar. II., 242.

It may be well to remove another error, which is more or less prevalent in the neighbourhood, namely, that the Church of S. James was the old Church of the Priory. S. James's was a chapelry of the Vicarage of S. Mary Magdalene, and was not made a distinct and independent Parish until some time subsequent to the Dissolution. Its truly venerable and stately Tower,—which in real dignity, simple sublimity, and architectural excellence far surpasses in the judgment of the writer its later and more pretentious neighbour, magnificent as that was, which has recently been demolished,—yet happily endures to inspire men with respect for the ability of their forefathers, and, although it has no claim to be considered the appendage of the grand and sumptuous Conventual Church, should be loved and guarded as a priceless treasure, all the more invaluable from its now standing alone.

If we regard the influence of the place, as a member of the vast ecclesiastical establishment of the land, we may trace numerous evidences of the exercise of a power the very reverse of contemptible. The Priors of the House were among the foremost of their fellows. As we have repeatedly observed in the previous pages, they bore their share and played their part in the great events of a series of generations, and those among some of the grandest and most interesting in our national annals. It appears that they were usually elected from the superior officers of the community. At the resignation, for example, of Prior Walter de Grateley, John de Kyngesbury his successor was Subprior, and Walter Cook who followed him was cellarer. The election was always conducted with great regularity. After the burial of the deceased Prior, the patron was solicited to issue his licence for the choice of a successor. This obtained, the Convent proceeded to their solemn duty. The mass de Spiritu Sancto was celebrated in their Conventual Church, after which the Canons were summoned to the Chapter House. The patron's letter was then read, the votes were taken, and, on the majority being declared, Te Deum was sung, the elect was conducted to the high altar, and his election solemnly declared. The confirmation of him by the Bishop to his dignity followed shortly after, and his conventual reign began.

It will not be amiss, as the detail has been so considerable, if I place before the reader in a consecutive series a list of the Priors, referring him for further particulars to our previous pages. I am happy to add—although I have not usually drawn attention to the wholesale omissions and errors of the few previous writers on this strangely overlooked and forgotten House—that several of these dignitaries now find their place in the assemblage for the first time.

1. Stephen occurs as a witness in documents of 1159, 1174, 1189, &c.

2. Robert, in a document of 1197.

3. John, in documents of 1204, &c.

4. John, in documents of 1313 and 1314.

5. Stephen de Picoteston died in 1325.

6. Ralph de Culmstock was elected on the 6th, received assent on the 11th, and was confirmed Prior on the 23rd of January, 1326; was one of the sub-collectors of the Tenths, 1330; was commissioned to purify his church, 1332; was summoned to the council in London, 1332; was appointed a collector of the Tenths, 1334; and resigned office on the 22nd of March, 1339.

7. Robert de Messingham was elected on the 19th of April, 1339; and died in March, 1346.

8. Thomas Cok was elected on the 30th of March,

received assent on the 4th of April, and did homage on the 16th of June, 1346; and was cited to the church of S. Mary le Bow on the 21st of July, 1353.

9. Thomas de Pederton died in November, 1361.

10. Walter de Grateley received assent on the 17th of January, 1362; and resigned office on the 29th of December, 1377.

11. John de Kyngesbury was elected in April, and received assent on the 1st of May, 1378; and died on the 5th of November, 1391.

12. Walter Coke was elected on the 21st and received assent on the 27th of November, 1391; occurs in 1406; and died in January, 1408.

13. Robert Newton was elected on the 18th, and confirmed Prior on the 31st of January, 1408; occurs in 1409; and died on the 12th of August, 1413.

14. Thomas de Ufcolme was elected on the 1st, and confirmed Prior on the 2nd of September, 1413; was summoned to convocation in November, 1415; and presented a clerk to Clannaborough, on the 5th of October, 1429.

15. Thomas Benet was summoned to convocation in 1438.

16. Richard Gleno occurs in June, 1449; was summoned to convocation the same year; presented a clerk to Lydiard S. Laurence, 1470; and died on the 31st of January, 1476.

17. John Asshe was nominated his successor on the 27th of February, and received assent on the 17th of March, 1476.

18. John Prous occurs Prior in 1492 and 1497; received permission from Pope Alexander VI. to use the pontifical insignia, on the 4th of May, 1499; was presented to Lydeyard S. Laurence in 1502; presented clerks to S.

Mary Magdalene and Ninehead, 1508; was summoned to convocation, 1509; resigned office on the 3rd of February, 1514; and died, 1519.

19. Nicholas Peper was elected on the 23rd of February, 1514; was summoned to convocation the same year; was again summoned to convocation, 1515; presented a clerk to Thurloxton in August, 1523; and died on the 26th of the following September.

20. William Yorke was nominated Prior on the 19th of November, 1523.

21. William Wyllyams, or Andrewes, was the last Prior, of whom more will be detailed presently.

In 1377, John de Kyngesbury was Sub-prior, Walter Cook was Cellarer, Peter Ilmynstre was Sacristan, and John Cley was Precentor.

In continuation of these registers, and again referring the reader to previous pages for the various details, we notice that the Incumbents presented by the Prior and Convent to their benefices may be classed as follows. The lists, though necessarily imperfect, are valuable so far as they extend.

Incumbents of Taunton S. Mary Magdalene:—Simon de Lym, 1308; Richard de Poterne, 1322; Robert Pippecote, 1346; William atte Stone, 1349; Hugh Thomas, ———; William Bury, 1508. William atte Halle was Curate of S. James's and Stapelgrove, in 1353; and Richard Pomerey was Chaplain of S. Andrew's Chantry in the Church of S. Mary Magdalene, in 1444.

Incumbents of Kingston:—Richard de Pym, 1339; William de Ayssheleigh, 1344; Robert Good, ———; Richard Pleysse, 1511.

Incumbents of Lydiard S. Laurence:—Thomas de Columbrugg, ———; John de Kyngesbury, 1318; Simon de Fareweye, 1351; Thomas Drayton, ———; John Valens,

1452 (?); John Vowell, ——; John Prowse, 1502; John North, 1519; Robert Morwent, 1521.

Incumbents of Pitminster:—John Stede, 1341; Robert Cox, 1349; Richard Heryng, 1350; Simon de Cherde, 1351; Richard Mader, ——; William Mors, 1509; Thomas Wyse, 1520; James Henton, ——; William Wyneyard, 1527.

Incumbents of Dulverton:—Adam, ——; Thomas Flour, 1332; Hugh Lovegeer, 1349; John Edyngton, ——; Hugh Thomas, 1504; Peter Druet, 1508; William Bowreman, ——; John Slocock, 1524.

Incumbents of Combflory:—John de Kyngesbury, 1317; Thomas de Columbrugg, 1318; Geoffrey de Reyny, 1336; William de Modbury, 1349; John Prows, ——; John Baker, 1502; John Hyll, 1514.

Incumbents of Ninehead:—Richard le Bellringer, 1315; William Wysman, 1349; John Cryspyn, 1350; William Esch, 1350; William Donckyn, 1362; John Prous, ——; John Samson, 1501; John Trygge, 1507; Thomas Cokysden, 1508.

Incumbents of Thurloxton:—William de la Pytte, 1318; Gilbert, ——; Walter de Quenton, 1333; Reginald Marchall, 1347; Ralph Mareschal, 1349; William de Esech, 1362; John Symmys, ——; Thomas Symons, 1505; John Hogans, 1523; James Dowdyng, 1530.

Incumbents of Runnington:—William de Lydeford, ——; William Syward, 1326; John Cryspyn, 1349; William Wysman, 1350; William Wysman, 1362; John Newman, 1408; Robert Tedworth, ——; Robert Huet, 1522; John Hill, 1526.

The possessions of the Priory were for the most part in its immediate neighbourhood, a great portion of which was represented, as we have already noticed, in the pages of its ample cartulary. Among the more distant, although situated in the same county, were the valuable manor of Dulverton, which has so often been the subject of remark, the vills of Broggelesnole and Levercote and the hamlets of Telchete and la Merse, mentioned in the Perambulation of the Forest of Exmore, dated on the 22nd of March, 1342,* and the lands of Staverdale and Thorn-Coffin. In Devon there were the Churches of Willand and Clannaborough, and lands at Woodham, Godesaltr, Prior Merston, and Monksbeare. In Dorset there was Buckham-Weston. The whole constituted a spacious domain, the beauty and fertility of which it would have been hard to parallel.

With regard to the revenues of the House, which were proportionably considerable, some curious information may be offered. At the time of the Valor of Pope Nicholas IV., 1288-1291, the temporalties belonging to the Community within the Archdeaconry of Taunton were taxed, according to the Memoranda Roll of the 34th of Edward III., 1360, at cccxvs.; namely, Nyenhide, xxvs.; Spaxton, xiijs. 4d.; Dulverton, xxvjs.; Thornlockeston, lxxs. viijd.; Northperton, xxs.; Stoke, xxxs.; Westmonekton, xs.; Lydiard S. Laurence, xxs.; and Esse Prior's, cs. Some time subsequently a commission was issued, bearing date the 26th of January, 1341, and addressed to certain Assessors and Venditors, who were thereby instructed to levy the Ninth of corn, wool, and lambs in every parish, for the maintenance of the king's wars and the good keeping of his realm, according to the aforesaid Valor. They were directed to take inquisition upon oath of certain jurors resident in every parish as to the true value of the Ninth. The returns which they made state at the same time the

* Per. For. de Exmore, ad Adam. de Domerham, Hist. Glast. j. 193, 194. Appendix, No. CLVI.

amount of the former tax, and, if the Ninth did not equal
that sum, the reason of such deficiency. In the roll just
quoted, to which also reference has been cursorily made in
a previous portion of this memoir, the Prior is recorded to
have objected to the amount at which he was rated, which
was no less than the sum of cix*s*. vij*d*. ob (halfpenny).
Upon examination of the return, it was discovered that this
amount was computed as follows :—Northcory, ij*s*. iiij*d* ;
Nycnhide, xiij*s*. iiij*d*; Bishop's Lydierd, vj*s*. viij*d*.; Spaxton, v*s*.; Dulverton, xij*s*.; Thorlokeston, xxvj*s*. viij*d*.;
Pedirton, iiij*s*.; Stokepire, v*s*. vj*d*. ; Monkcton, xij*s*. vj*d*.;
Lydierd S. Laurence, xj*s*. vij*d*. ob. ; Esso Prior's, x*s*. Reference was then made to the roll of the 20th of Edward
I., or the Taxation of Pope Nicholas, and the temporalties were stated as there set forth ; when it appeared that
the Prior and his predecessors paid a Tenth for all and
singular of these temporalties. It did not, however, appear
that the Prior had then any temporalties taxed in Northcory
and Bishop's Lydiard. Accordingly, he stated his willing-
ness to pay the sum demanded of ix*s*. on these two proper-
ties, but that he had no others on which an assessment might
lawfully be made. After a lengthened investigation, the
Prior appeared in Easter Term in the Court of Exchequer,
when an inquisition was exhibited, taken at Somerton in
the presence of the said Prior by John de Hundesmore
his attorney, on the Monday in the fifth week in Lent,
1361, in which the jurors on their oath declared that the
Prior had no other temporalties save those which had been in
the possession of his House in the year 1291, and which
were then taxed, except one carucate of land and a rent of
fifty shillings with its appurtenances in Dulverton, which
Prior Robert de Messingham (or Cressingham) had pur-
chased for himself and his successors ; that the value of the

Ninth from that property was xld.; and that Monketon and Westmonekton, Pedirton and Northperton, and Stoke Pirye and Stoke, were respectively two names for one and the same place. It was thereupon decided that the Prior should pay the aforesaid sums of ixs. for Northcory and Bishop's Lydeyerd, and of xld. for Dulverton, and that he should be relieved and quit of the further demand of iiijli. xvijs. iiijd. ob., at which he had been illegally assessed.*

These notices furnish us among other information both with the relative value of the estates at one and the same time, and with their comparative value at different periods.

Monastic annals are by no means silent in regard of those who bore the name of the House, either perhaps from some early connection with it, or from having been born in the adjoining town. William de Tanton was Prior of Winchester in 1249; John de Tanton was Canon of Wells, 1247; Gilbert de Tanton was Almoner of Glastonbury, 1274; John de Taunton was at the same time Abbat of Glastonbury; Walter de Tanton was Abbat of Glastonbury, 1322; John de Tanton was vicar of Northcory, 1328; Robert de Tanton was prebendary of Wivelescomb in the Church of Wells, 1333; Nicholas de Tanton was vicar of Brompton Regis, 1348; and John de Taunton was Abbat of Cirencester, in 1440. This list could be greatly extended if necessary. But it is more than sufficient to show that ecclesiastics who were connected, as at least is probable, with the Priory or the town, attained during a long series of years to some of the highest dignities which this and other dioceses included within their pale.

That one of the accomplishments of a monastery here

* Memorand. Rot. 24 Edw. III. Trin. Appendix, No. LXXXIII.

flourished in perfection, it is probable that I possess a very interesting proof. I have in my collection a Psalter, with a litany of the Saints and other prayers, written in the latter part of the thirteenth or the beginning of the fourteenth century, most beautifully executed and undoubtedly by an English scribe. A calendar is prefixed, singularly valuable, together with the litany, for the number of English Saints which it records. Nearly at the end of the book, which is of what would now be called small duodecimo size, and has two hundred and forty three leaves, is an illumination consisting of a scroll on which is inscribed "Jon Taunton. MS." It is not unlikely that this charming volume, unless it were the work of the famous Abbat of Glastonbury himself, who was a great lover of books, was produced in the scriptorium of Taunton Priory; and, if so, the House had no reason to be ashamed of its penman. That the community were possessed of a library of some importance is evident from the fact that Leland, who visited the Priory within a short period of the suppression, although, as usual, he is unhappily silent about the edifice itself, noticed three uncommon books in the collection of the Canons, the "Chronicon Ivonis," "Philaretus de Pulsibus," and "Theophilus de Urinis,"* representatives of the literature and science of the mediæval age.

I am also in possession of a very interesting relic which was found about thirty-five years ago, during the process of removing an accumulation of mud in the bed of the Tone, within a few hundred yards from the site of the Priory, and which has been in my custody for the far greater part of the intervening period. It is a leaden bulla of Pope Sixtus IV., who occupied the chair of S.

---

* Lel. Collect., tom. III., p. 153.

BULLA OF POPE SIXTUS IV.,

Found in the River Tone near Taunton Priory.

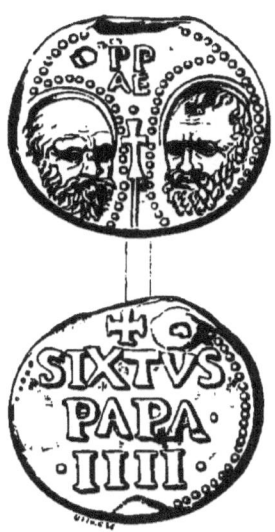

(*Actual Size*).

Drawn and Engraved for the REV. THOMAS HUGO'S
"*History of Taunton Priory.*"

GIRDLE ORNAMENT,

Found on the site of Taunton Priory.

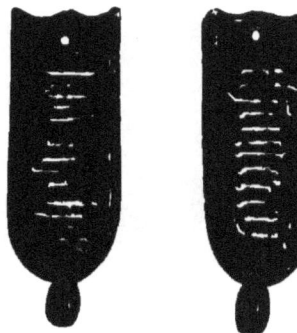

(*Actual Size*).

Drawn and Engraved for the REV. THOMAS HUGO'S
"*History of Taunton Priory.*"

KNIFE HANDLE,

Found on the site of Taunton Priory.

(Actual Size).

Drawn and Engraved for the Rev. Thomas Hugo's
"History of Taunton Priory."

Peter from 1471 to 1484, and was originally attached to a document not improbably addressed to Taunton Priory or its Prior. [*See the engraving.*] On the purport of the missive it would of course be vain to speculate.

For another object of interest connected with the House I have to thank my old friend Henry Norris, Esq., late of South Petherton, who most kindly presented it to me. It is a brass ornament which formed the termination of a leathern girdle, and is a work of the fifteenth century. On one side are the words 𝔥𝔢 𝔪𝔢𝔯𝔠𝔶, and on the other 𝔩𝔞𝔡𝔶 𝔥𝔢𝔩𝔭𝔢. It was found on the site of the Priory in the year 1812, and was sold at the time of its discovery to his learned father. [*See the figures.*] About the same time and in the same locality was found the haft of a knife in morse-ivory, which was similarly offered for sale and is at present also in my possession. It is of the latter part of the fifteenth century, and consists of a group of three figures, probably intended for Faith, Hope, and Justice, which are surmounted by a couchant lion. Faith is represented with a staff, Hope with an anchor and a bird, and Justice with a sword and a pair of scales. [*See the figures.*] During the last ten years a few coins have been offered to me for sale, with the special recommendation of having been discovered on the same site, or in the immediate neighbourhood, comprising pennies of Henry II., Edward III., and Richard II., and a groat and shilling of Henry VIII. These, however, as it was well known that I was interested in the locality, and as the circumstances of the alleged discoveries were not free from suspicion, I receive with considerable hesitation, and tender a word of caution to those of my readers to whom similar objects may hereafter be exhibited.

Up to this period we have seen the noble House which

L

is the subject of our present research rising hastily during the first part of its existence into a position of wealth and power, and then for a series of generations dispensing with a high and liberal hand the manifold blessings of which it was the favoured depository. Age after age it has been entering into the ecclesiastical life of England, an integral portion of the mighty whole, and making its presence felt in conformity with the great purposes for which it had received its being. A change has now arrived. By this time Taunton had received its last Prior, and the House its last legitimate master. From this point, then, the spectator must be invited to look upon a far different picture. There is from the nature of things an unhappy necessity forced upon the writer, who endeavours to rescue from oblivion the annals of any one of our old Religious Houses. The histories which are the result of such reverent care differ oftentimes in all possible ways, so far as the records of good deeds can be unlike each other; but the last chapter of the tale, the last fearful scene, is the same in all. The same demoniac passions, the same sacrilegious wills, the same accursed hands, prompted the outrage and perpetrated the crime. Glastonbury, and Taunton, and Muchelney, and Cleeve, and Buckland, and Crewkerne, and Montacute, and Athelney, and hundreds of others—all tell of the same remorseless tyrant, the same fawning band of greedy courtiers, and the same atrocious spirit of wrong, robbery, and murder, all the more abominable and disgusting from the pretence of religion with which it was invested.

Little more than a year had elapsed after the annexation of Staverdale to Taunton, when the opposition of the clergy to the king's matrimonial speculations brought about the severance of the Anglican Church from the spiritual

supremacy of the See of Rome. Inasmuch as the Pope
refused to sanction the divorce of the monarch's outraged
wife, and to permit him to elevate one of her waiting-
women to her place, Henry, who appeared to think that
every thing whether of heaven or earth was created solely
for his peculiar gratification, resolved to break off all connexion with him, and to declare himself pope within his
own unhappy dominions. We shall entirely miss the real
meaning of the affair unless we keep this circumstance
prominently in view. It was for his own loathsome purposes that his public acts were originated and carried out.
The great body of the clergy, who were known to be
antagonistic to his wishes, was therefore to be coerced into
seeming approval, and the statute which declared the
Royal Supremacy was the instrument by which it was
effected. The clauses of the declaration which the Religious Houses were called upon to make distinctly prove
that the confirmation of the divorce was the leading result
intended, and that the renunciation of the pope was a
childish act of mere retaliation for his opposition to the
despot's will. The declaration itself was a carefully prepared document, a blank form of which was carried to every
community, with spaces left for the insertion of the name
and style of the particular House, and room at the conclusion
for the signatures of the brethren. It sets out with some
fulsome assertions of their duty to the unscrupulous sovereign who so little regarded his duty to them, and of the
sincere, entire, and perpetual devotion, faith, observance,
honor, worship, and reverence which they were prepared
most willingly to render to him. It then proceeds to
announce that the Heads of the House in question with
one mouth, voice, and unanimous consent and assent,
profess, attest, and faithfully promise and vow for them-

selves and their successors, all and singular, that they will
pay entire, inviolate, sincere, and perpetual fidelity, observance and obedience to the king and to Anne the queen his
wife, and to his offspring by the same Anne then begotten
or to be so: that they will at all possible times notify the
same to the people: that Henry is the head of the Church
of England: that the Bishop of Rome is to be considered
of no higher dignity than any other bishop in his own
diocese: that no one either in private or in public assem-
blies, or in his prayers, shall call the Bishop of Rome by
the title of pope or supreme pontiff, but by the name of
the Bishop of Rome or of the Roman Church: that the
laws and decrees of the king shall be maintained, and that
those of the Bishop of Rome shall be renounced: that the
Catholic and Orthodox faith shall be duly preached: that
in public prayers mention shall first be made of the king,
as the supreme head of the Church of England, then of
Queen Anne with her family, and lastly of the Archbishops
of Canterbury and York, with the other orders of the
clergy: concluding with an oath of obligation and faithful
and perpetual observance of all and singular the matters
aforesaid.

Such was the compulsory and unsparing declaration.
It was made in the Chapter House of Taunton Priory,
and sealed with the common seal, on the 15th of Septem-
ber, 1534, in the 26th year of "the most invincible prince
Henry VIII." In the attesting witnesses, fifteen in number,
we are furnished with the names of the entire community.
They were William Wyllyams, Prior, William Gregory,
Sub-prior, Antony Whytt, William Bayle, Nicholas Bernm,
Thomas Dale, John Heyward, William Culron, John
Cokeram, John Dyght, John Warryn, Richard Fynsham,
William Cobock, William Brynchmede, and William

SEAL OF TAUNTON PRIORY,

From an Impression attached to the Surrender in the Augmentation Office.

(Actual Size).

Drawn and Engraved for the REV. THOMAS HUGO'S
"*History of Taunton Priory.*"

Bleche.* An impression in red wax is appendant of the Common Seal of the Priory. It is of early character, of the vesica form, and represents the Apostles SS. Peter and Paul standing under crocketed canopies with a diapered background. The architectural peculiarities are indicative of the age of Edward I., and therefore exactly harmonize with those which prevailed at the period of the erection of the Conventual Church. The Apostles are represented with their characteristic insignia, the former with his keys in his left, and a church, to which reference has already been made, in his right hand, and the latter with his sword. The legend reads, 𝔖. 𝔖𝔠𝔞𝔫𝔠𝔱𝔦. 𝔞𝔭𝔬𝔰𝔱𝔬𝔩𝔬𝔯. 𝔭𝔢𝔱 * * * 𝔗. 𝔭𝔞𝔲𝔩𝔦. * 𝔞𝔫𝔱𝔬𝔫𝔦𝔢𝔰𝔦𝔰. 𝔢 * * * * *.—Sigillum Sanctorum Apostolorum Petri et Pauli Tantoniensis Ecclesiæ. (*See the figure.*)

The declaration of the king's supremacy was the first step towards the spoliations that ensued. The tyrant discovered his power and acted accordingly. Those that refused the declaration, as Bp. Fisher, Sir Thomas More and others, were sent to the block or the halter, and those who complied with it were but reserved for future vengeance. Things did not, indeed could not, long remain as they were. To enable the king to maintain his position as "supreme head on earth of the Church of England," it was presently enacted that every possessor of any ecclesiastical dignity, office or place should surrender to him the first-fruits, revenues and profits for one year, and, further, should pay to him every year a tenth of all his revenues, emoluments and profits, and that the first payment should be made at the Feast of the Nativity, 1535. Hereupon Commissioners were appointed by Parliament to enquire

---

* Ex Autograph. in Off. Reo. olim Augment. Appendix, No. CLVII.

into and report upon the value of all ecclesiastical possessions throughout the country. This was promptly carried into effect, and the returns which were made by these officers constitute the well-known "Valor Ecclesiasticus," in which they were digested and presented to both houses.

The "Valor" of Taunton Priory furnishes us with a complete view of the possessions of the House immediately before the suppression. It shows also what sums were paid to various clerical and lay persons, bailiffs, sheriffs, auditors, and other civil officers, the charges due to the chief Lords, the amount spent in alms by reason of any foundation or ordinance, with the names of the parties so commemorated, &c. We are thus presented with a most lively picture of the rights on the one hand and the liabilities on the other of one of the greater monasteries during its last few years of place and power.

As the return is necessarily of so great importance and interest, I have thought proper to give it in translation, and with its minute details more intelligibly represented than as they stand in the original. The amounts, however, still figure in their ancient form, as I was unwilling to modernize my authority when there was little or nothing to be gained by the alteration. In studying the account we should not forget either the easy terms which monastic tenants notoriously enjoyed, or the immense increase in the value of property from those times to our own, considerations of the greatest importance in enabling us to arrive at a due appreciation of the position of the House. It may also be premised that the record includes not only the possessions already noticed as donations to the Priory at various earlier periods, but those also which were lately added by the union with it of the Priory of Staverdale.

HOUSE AND PRIORY OF TAUNTON.

Declaration of the Extent and Annual Value of all and singular the Lands, and Tenements, and other Possessions, with the Tithes, Oblations, and all other Issues of the divers Benefices and Chapels belonging and appropriated to the aforesaid Priory, in the time of William Andrewes, now Prior thereof.

ESSE.—(Ash Priors.)

Value in assized Rents of the Customary Tenants	vij^{li} iij^s ix^d		
Demesne Lands ..	x^{li} iij^s ij^d	xvj^{li} xviij^s xj^d	
Out of this a rent, annually, To William Frances	vij^s		xx^{li} xj^s xj^d
To the Lord of the Manor of Bp's Lydeyarde	xij^d		
So now clear			
Perquisites of the Courts and other Casualties, in common years,	xxx^s		
Fines of lands	xliij^s		

WESTOWE.

Assized Rents of the Customary Tenants ..	lxxj^s vj^d		
Demesne Lands ..	xlix^s x^d		
Out of this, annually, To the turn of the Sheriff of Somerset ..	xij^d	cxviij^s iiij^d	vij^{li} xj^s viij^d
To the Lord of the Hundred of Williton	ij^s		
So now clear			
Perquisites of the Courts and other Casualties	iij^s iiij^d		
Fines of lands	xxx^s		

MIDDELTON.

Rents both of Free and of Customary Tenants lxij˙ vj^d	} xj^li xiiij˙ vj^d	} xij^li –˙ xiiij^d
Demesne Lands .. xij˙		
Demesne Lands in the hand of the Lord x^li		
Out of this, The fee of Stephen Stroude, bailiff of the same .. xl˙		
So now clear		
Perquisites of the Courts and other Casualties .. .. vj˙ viij^d		

WILLOND.

Assized Rents of the Customary Tenants vij^li ix˙ x^d	} xv^li iiij˙ vij^d	} xviij^li iij˙ vij^d
Demesne Lands vij^li xviij˙ iiij^d		
Out of this annually, To the Lord of the Manor of Holberton iij˙ vj^d		
So now clear		
Perquisites of the Courts and other Casualties .. .. ix˙		
Fines of Lands .. .. l˙		

THURLOXSTON.

Value in Rents of Free as of Customary Tenants .. ix^li –˙ xx^d ob.	} xiiij^li ij˙ iij^d
Demesne Lands cxiiij˙ ob.	
Out of which there is an annual payment, To the Master of the Hospital of Brygewater .. .. xij˙	

To the turn of the Sheriff of Somerset	iij^d	
To the Lord of the Hundred of Androyfelde	xij^d	xviij^{li} ij^s viij^d
To the Lord of the Manor of Dunster	iij^d	

So now clear

Perquisites of the Courts and other Casualties	.. ..	xx^s
Fines of lands	.. ..	lx^s iiij^d

BLACKEDON.

Assised Rents of the Customary Tenants	.. .. iiij^{li} xvij^d ob.	
Demesne Lands	.. .. xxvij^s	cix^s ix^d ob.
Perquisites of the Courts and other Casualties	.. xvj^d	

TODRUGGE.

Assised Rents of the Customary Tenants	.. .. cxiiij^s x^d	
Demesne Lands	.. .. xxiij^s iij^d	vj^{li} xix^s v^d
Perquisites of the Courts and other Casualties	.. .. xvj^d	

DULVERTON DEMESNE.

Assised Rents of the Free as of the Customary Tenants	.. vij^{li} v^s x^d	
Demesne lands	.. .. vij^{li} iiij^s ix^d	
Out of which, annually,		
To the Lord of Dunster	.. xiij^d	
To the Lord of Hawkerige	ij^s ij^d	xlvij^s iiij^d
A pension to the Prior of Bustelham Mountegue	vj^{li} xiij^s iiij^d	

A pension to a chantry priest
of Donyatte .. lxvj˙ viijᵈ
The fee of William Glosse,
bailiff of the same .. xl˙
So now clear

DULVERTON PARSONAGE.

Assised Rents of the Free as of Customary
Tenants, clear .. .. .. xjˡⁱ iiij˙ vᵈ

DULVERTON BAILIWICK.

Assised Rents of the Cus-
tomary Tenants .. xl˙ xjᵈ ⎫ lˢ xjᵈ
Demesne Lands .. xˢ ⎭
Perquisites of the Courts and other ⎱ xijˡⁱ iiˢ xjᵈ
Casualties .. .. lxˢ
Fines of lands .. .. vjˡⁱ xijˢ

PIXSTON.

Assised Rents of the Cus-
tomary Tenants .. cˢ vjᵈ
Demesne Lands xˡⁱ
Out of which annually,
To the Bp. of Winches-   xiiijˡⁱ xviijˢ xᵈ   xvˡⁱ ijˢ ijᵈ
ter, a chief rent, .. xijᵈ
To the Abbat of Glas-
tonbury .. viijᵈ
So now clear
Perquisites of the Courts and other
Casualties .. .. iijˢ iiijᵈ

TAUNTON EXTRA PORTAM.

Assised Rents of the Cus-
tomary Tenants xijˡⁱ vijˢ xᵈ ob.
Perquisites of the Courts   xiiijˡⁱ xiiijˢ vjᵈ ob.
and other Casualties vjˢ viijᵈ
Fines of lands .. xxˢ

CANON STREET.

Assised Rents of the Customary Tenants	xxvij^{li} xij^s vj^d	
Sale of works ..	vij^s vj^d	xxviij^{li}
Perquisites of the Courts and other Casualties	xxx^s	
Fines of lands	xxij^s	

Total: xxx^{li} xii^s

FONS GEORGIJ.—(Wilton).

Rents of the Customary Tenants ..	lix^s	iiij^{li} xxij^d
Sale of works ..	xxij^s x^d	
Perquisites of the Courts and other Casualties	iij^s iiij^d	

Total: iiij^{li} v^s ij^d

GAULDON.

Rents of the Customary Tenants, with works	vj^{li} x^s vj^d	
Demesne Lands ..	iiij^{li}	x^{li} v^s v^d
Out of which, annually, To the Lord of the Manor of Pyligh, a chief rent	v^s j^d	
So now clear		
Perquisites of the Courts and other Casualties	iij^s iiij^d	

Total: x^{li} viij^s ix^d

THURLEBERE.

Assised Rents of the Customary Tenants	iiij^{li} j^d	
Perquisites of the Courts and other Casualties	xx^d	
Fines of lands	xiij^s iiij^d	

Total: iiij^{li} xv^s j^d

KYNGISHILL.

Rents of the Free as of the Customary Tenants	xliij^s ij^d	
Out of which, annually, To the Lord of Strengiston for a chief rent	iiij^d	
So now clear		

Total: xlij^s x^d

WHITEHULL.—(Withiel.)

Rents of the Customary Tenants, clear .. xxxj˙

STAFFORDELL.

Annual Rent of the farm of the Manor, as by the Indenture of Nicholas Fitz-James .. .. c˙

WYNCAULTON.

Assised Rents of the Customary Tenants viij^li viij˙ j^d
Out of which, annually,
  To the Lord Henry Daubeny .. x^d
  So now clear
} viij^li vij˙ iij^d

Perquisites of the Courts and other Casualties .. .. vj˙ viij^d
Fines of lands .. .. xx^d

} viij^li xv˙ vij^d

RUNDEHILL.

Assised Rent of the firm of the Manor ix^li
Out of which, annually,
  To the turn of the Sheriff of Somerset xv^d
  A chief rent to John Boneham, Esq. iij˙
  A chief rent to the heirs of Chalket for land in Cleyanger .. xij^d
  So now clear

} viij^li xiiij˙ ix^d

BAROW.

Assised Rents of the Customary Tenants viij^li vj˙ vj^d
Out of which, annually,
  To the Lord Abbat of Glastonbury, for lands in Batcombe .. xiiij^d
  To the heirs of Rodney for land in Lovyngton xvij^d
  So now clear
} viij^li iij˙ xj^d

Perquisites of the Courts and other Casualties .. .. v˙

} viij^li viij˙ xj^d

BRUETON.

Rents of Free and of Customary Tenants	xij^{li} xiij^s v^d	
Out of which, annually,		
To the Lord of the Hundred of Cattisaishe, as for a chief rent	xviij^d	
To the Abbat of Bruton	xij^d	
To the Lord of Norton Farrys	xij^d	x^{li} viij^s xj^d
To the Lord Henry Daubeny, for a chief rent for land in Bryggewater	xij^d	
For the fee of Egidius Slade, steward of the same	xx^s	
For the fee of William Love, bailiff of the same	xx^s	

x^{li} xix^s xj^d

So clear

Perquisites of the Courts and other Casualties		ix^s iiij^d
Fines of lands		xx^d

THORNECOFFYN.

Rents of free and of Customary Tenants, per annum, clear .. . .. iiij^{li} iiij^d

RENTS OF CERTAIN PARCELS OF LAND.

For one burgage in Langporte	v^s	
Of certain Tenements in Athelbury	xiij^s iiij^d	
Certain rents in Canon Street	xxxiij^s	
Caplond	xx^s	viij^{li} ij^s iiij^d
Grassecrofte	xxx^s	
Next the Chapel, Taunton	xj^s iiij^d	
Oldeclyff	v^s	

Plaistrete	xiij˚ iiijᵈ	
Briggewater	iiij˚	
Taunton	xiiij˚	
Certain Rent of John Alwyn ..	xiij˚ iiijᵈ	

RECEIPTS.

For a certain annual rent from the Lord of the Manor of Hockecombe	xxᵈ	
For a similar rent from the Vicarage of Kyngeston	xv˚	iiijˡⁱ v˚ viijᵈ
For a similar rent from the Rectory of Clowyngborow ..	iiij˚	
From the Rector of Orchard, for a similar rent	v˚	
From the Vicarage of Dulverton, for a similar rent	lx˚	

DEMESNE LANDS NEXT THE PRIORY HOUSE.

From the Issues and Annual Value of certain Demesne Lands, in the Lord's hand, and lying by and about the Priory House, by the oath of four honest and lawful men	cxj˚ ixᵈ

SALE OF THE TITHES OF GRAIN AND MEADOWS, AS BELOW.

Tithes of Corn of Kyngeston and Cothelston .. .. xiiijˡⁱ		
Tithes of Corn of Hamwode, parcel of the Parish of Trull .. vijˡⁱ	xvjᵈ	
Pallyngisfelde and Holeford ..	c˚	
Wyncaulton .. .. viijˡⁱ		lxiiijˡⁱ x˚ ijᵈ
Nynched .. .. vjˡⁱ xvij˚		
Dulverton .. .. xijˡⁱ	x˚	
Tithes of Meadows of Langford and Cleyhill	ij˚	

TAUNTON PRIORY.   95

Tithes of the Meadows of Robert At-mershe .. xiiij^d
Tithes of Corn of Thurlebere ix^{li} vj^s viij^d
Tithes of the Rectory of Oterforde .. .. xxxij^s

In all
ISSUES AND PROFITS OF THE TITHES OF GRAIN, WITH OTHER TITHES AND CASUALTIES OF CHAPELS, AS BELOW.

The Tithes of Grain of the Parish of S. Mary Magdalene, with the Oblations and other casualties .. xxxj^{li} xij^s xj^d
The Tithes of Grain of Corffe, Pitmyster, and Trull, with the Oblations and other casualties .. .. xij^{li} iij^s v^d
The Tithes of Grain of the Parish of S. James's and Stapulgrave, with the Oblations and other casualties xiiij^{li} ix^s xj^d
The Tithes of Grain of Whitehull, with the Oblations and other casualties .. ix^{li} vj^s iiij^d
The Tithes of Grain of Esse, with the Oblations and other casualties .. .. viij^{li} xiij^s v^d } cxij^{li} xiij^s j^d
The Tithes of Grain of Trulle, with the Oblations and other casualties .. .. vj^{li} ix^d
The Tithes of Grain of [Bishop's] Hulle, with the Oblations and other casualties .. .. .. xvj^{li} xv^s vj^d

The Tithes of Grain of Russheton, with the Oblations and other casualties ... x{li} xvijs iijd
The Tithes of Grain of Wilton, with the Oblations and other casualties ... ... lxxiij{s} vijd

    In all

Sum total of the value as well of all the Temporals as of the Spirituals aforesaid } ccccxxxviij{li} viijs xd

  From this are to be deducted,

ALLOWANCES, PENSIONS, AND STIPENDS, AS BELOW.

For a perpetual annual Pension to the Vicar of Taunton ... xx{li}
For the Stipends of divers Chaplains serving the Chapels, as above,—namely
 To John Selake, chaplain of Esse   cxiij{s} iiijd
 To John Sabbyn, chaplain of Trull   vj{li} xiijs iiijd
 To John Hare, chaplain of Hill Bishop's ... ... vj{li}
 To John Stotte, chaplain of Russheton and Stoke ... vj{li} xiijs iiijd
 To John Baillyff, chaplain of Corffe   c{s} } iiij{xx}·iij{li}
 To Thomas Cocks, chaplain of Wilton ... ... c{s}
 To William Badcock, chaplain of S. James's ... ... vj{li} xiijs iiijd
 To Humfrey Bradley, chaplain of Whitehull ... ... cvj{s} viijd
 To two Chaplains serving in the Church of Staffordell, according to the Ordination of William Yorke, late Prior of Taunton ... ... xvj{li}

PAYMENTS.

To the Church of Wells, as for an annual Pension from Staffordell	xxxiij^s iiij^d	⎫
To the Archdeacon of Taunton, for the rent of the aforesaid Churches and Chapels, annually	x^s iij^d	⎪
To the same, for procurations of the said Churches ...	l^s vij^d	⎪
An annual payment to the Rector of Hidon ...	xj^s vij^d	⎪
And Mouncketon, for a certain annual rent	vj^s viij^d	⎪
To the Bp. of Bath, for procurations	xxij^s	⎪
To the Bp. of Winchester, annually, for a chief rent of land in Grassecroft ...	vij^s	⎬ viij^{li} v^s viij^d
Baldewynsmede ...	vj^s viij^d	⎪
Kyngishill ...	iiij^d	⎪
and Tolond ...	ij^s	⎪
To the Archdeacon of Wells, annually, for procurations of the Church of Wyncaulton	ix^s x^d ob'	⎪
To the Bp. of Bath, for a certain rent issuing from the Rectory of Wyncaulton	iij^s iiij^d	⎪
Annual payment to the heirs of Beaumont as for a chief rent	ij^s	⎭

ALMS, FROM ORDINATIONS AND FOUNDERS.

In alms distributed, namely every Friday iij˚ iiij^d, to the poor, according to the Ordination of Bp. Henry Blesans, per annum ...	viij^{li} xiij˚ iiij^d
On the anniversary of the said Henry, in four quarterly payments of xiiij˚ ij^d each	lvj˚ viij^d
In alms given to the poor by the Ordination of William Gyfford, some time Bp. of Winchester, namely every Sunday xiiij^d ...	lx˚ viij^d
On the anniversary of Thomas Bekyngton, some time Bp. of Winchester	xxxix˚ iiij^d
According to the Ordination of John Aisshe of Staffordell	liij˚ iiij^d
Of the gifts of divers others, viz.	
Sir William Bondevyle ...	xxx˚
Thomas Mawdelyn, clerk ...	vj˚ viij^d
Margery Froment, widow ...	xiij˚ iiij^d
John Prescote	xiij˚ iiij^d
Walter Dowlynge ...	xxxiiij˚ viij^d
John Tose	xviij˚ iiij^d
Roger Hill	xxj˚
To seven poor persons residing near the Priory House, yearly	...xxxiiij˚
To four of the poor of Staffordell, by the Ordination of John Lord Zouche, John Lord Storton, William Yorke late Prior of Taunton, with others	xij^{li} iiij˚
On the anniversary of Baldowin, some time Bp. of Winchester, and on Maunday Thursday	xx˚ iiij^d

} xlj^{li} ix˚

SALARIES.

For the Salary of Sir Nicholas Wadam, Chief Steward of the Possessions aforesaid ...	cvj^s viij^d	⎫
For the Salary of Roger Yorke, Sergeant at law and Steward of the Manor of Staffordell with its members under the Conventual Seal ... ... iiij^{li}		⎬ xix^{li} v^s iiij^d
For the Salary of John Sooper, Auditor of the Possessions aforesaid	lxvj^s viij^d	
For the Salaries of divers officials, bailiffs, or collectors of certain rents, viz., Taunton Extra Portam, Canon Street, Staffordell, Fons Georgij, Gauldon, and other places, viz.,		
George Speake ...	lxvj^s viij^d	
Richard Grey ...	xl^s	
John Alford ...	xxv^s iiij^d	⎭
Sum of the Allowances ...	clij^{li} —^{s} —^{d}	
And so now there remains clear after all deductions	cciiij^{xx}vj^{li} viij^s x^d	
The Tenth from thence ...	xxviij^{li} xij^s x^d ob' q'.*	

We have here a balance-sheet for every part of the property, an exact return of income and expenditure, giving us without difficulty and at a single glance the proceeds of the several estates, the deductions to which they were subject, and the surplus that, after all the issues were

---

* Val. Eccl., vol. I., pp. 168, 169, 170. Appendix, No. CLVIII.

disbursed, still remained available for the provision and maintenance of the House.

In addition to the foregoing details the Valor furnishes us with the names of several other incumbents at the period of its formation, 1535.

William Bury was vicar of "Mawdelyn," which was valued at xx^{li} iij^s iiij^d.

In the same Church of S. Mary Magdalene there were several chantries, which are thus given, together with the names of their incumbents:—

The Chantry of the B. V. Mary—John Tuell.
    „   S. Nicholas—Robert Bailliffe.
    „   Jesus—John Wely.
    „   S. Andrew—John Harvye.
    „   Holy Trinity—Ralph Wylkyne.
    „   ————— Alexander Magote.
    „   S. Etheldreda—William Calowe.

At the same time Richard Jeffrey was Incumbent of Kyngeston with the Chapel of Cutston (Cothelstone), Edmund Turnor of Combefflory, Robert Morwent of Lydeard S. Laurence, John Marler of Nynchede, John Hill of Rownyngton, and William Wyneyard of Pytmyster.*

From our knowledge of the character of Henry, we may be well assured that the interval between the compilation of the Valor and the appropriation of the property which it represented was but a short and hardly perceptible step. As in a more ancient instance, the possession of the vineyard was too tempting an acquisition even for robbery and murder to offer any decided resistance to a tyrant's will. There was a difficulty, however, in his path which required some craft to overcome. And never was a more thoroughly

---

* Val. Eccl., vol. 1, pp. 171, 172, 173. Appendix, No. CLIX.

diabolical mode employed to obtain a shameless end than that to which his agents had resort. Sir Thomas More was hardly laid in his bloody grave when the infamous Cromwell proposed and carried into effect a so-called Visitation of the Religious Houses. When the avowed object was plunder, when the visitors, who were perfectly cognizant of their master's design, were sent for the very purpose of bringing an evil report upon the places which they inspected, when their own advantage was in exact ratio to the degree of criminality which they should succeed in attaching to their victims, and when they were rewarded in proportion to the insolence of their language and the atrocity of their behaviour, we need not wonder at the manner in which they conducted themselves, or at the returns which they made. The marvel is not that many reports were condemnatory but that any were of a different complexion. The official account of the visitation of Taunton Priory is not known to exist, but the date of it may be said to be at length recovered. It was doubtless on the 7th of August, 1537, that the reprobate priest Dr. Layton, the ever-ready calumniator and false accuser, whose name 1 mention for the purpose of affixing to him the infamy that he deserves, made his appearance at the monastery. This, the reader will recollect, is the date endorsed on the bull of Pope Alexander VI. already referred to, which among other documents passed under his inspection. His report we know not; though from such an inquisitor it could hardly be expected to be favourable.

In the previous year and during the course of these last mentioned enquiries came the dissolution of the lesser monasteries. The King attempted to seduce the minds of the more conscientious into at least tacit acquiescence with his plans, by promising to create

new Bishopricks in several of the larger dioceses.
Taunton among other places was selected for that honor.
On the Patent Roll of the 29th of his reign is a
mandate to Cranmer the Archbishop of Canterbury,
setting forth that the Bishop of Bath and Wells had
signified to him the need under which that diocese lay of
an active Suffragan, and that he had presented to him two
clerks, William Fynche late Prior of Bremar, and Richard
Walshe Prior of the Hospital of S. John Baptist of
Bridgewater, both in Priest's Orders, born in lawful matrimony, of lawful age, learned both in Spirituals and Temporals, and without Canonical impediment of any kind,
one of whom he had humbly and devoutly supplicated that
he would select for the high office. Further, that he, of
his special grace and mere motion, nominated William
Fynche, one of the aforesaid, to be Suffragan Bishop of
Taunton, and that he gives and confers on him the style,
title, and dignity of Suffragan Bishop. Finally, that he
requires the Archbishop to consecrate the said William
Fynche, thus nominated, and to confer on him Benediction, and all the Episcopal Insignia, and all and singular
other things which it belonged to his Pastoral Office to
confer. The missive was dated on the 25th of March,
1538.*

It is hardly necessary that I should inform my reader
that William Fynche was the last as well as the first
Bishop of Taunton.

The tempest was now all but come upon the greater and
richer Houses, and the enemy waited but time and opportunity to accomplish the work on which he was bent. It
is not my province, however, to dwell upon the general

---

* Pat. 29 Hen. VIII., p. 5, m. 23. Appendix, No. CLX.

preliminaries of the sad tragedy. I must hasten to the point at which Taunton Priory once more enters upon the scene.

The efforts of the Commissioners had been specially directed to induce the occupants of the Religious Houses to make a voluntary surrender of their possessions. Two modes were adopted for this desired result. On the one hand they were allured to comply by the promise of pensions, and on the other endeavours were made to frighten them into acquiescence by threats of the exposure of imaginary offences, and of the punishment of evils which had no foundation save in the minds of the visitors themselves. Some were proof against both of these manœuvres, and them, by trumped up charges of treason, or by the assertion of the concealment of their most valuable property, which if true was perfectly justifiable, they mercilessly tortured to the death. It has struck multitudes in later times with wonder, that the shameless attack on the Religious Houses was attended with so much apparent success; and it has been oftentimes inferred that the aims of the king and his courtiers must have been warmly seconded by the acquiescing verdict of the people at large. The contrary of this is the truth. The people looked upon the scenes that were disgracing the land with horror, consternation, and loathing, and every here and there, as in the West of England itself, rose in rebellion against the tyrant and his myrmidons. Nor—and let us not forget this—could the attempt have been successful, had it not been for the want of concentrated effort on the part of the clergy themselves. Singly they strove, and singly they were of course overcome.

The storm at length burst upon Taunton. It was on the 12th of February, 1539, that the Prior and Canons met in their Chapter House, and, in the presence of the Commissioner, John Tregonwell, unwillingly signed the instrument of Surrender. That it was done at the violation of every natural and reasonable feeling cannot, I presume, be questioned. It would indeed be impossible to frame a document, the terms of which could be more at variance with the minds of those who attached to it their hand and seal. Like the declaration of supremacy already described, it was prepared before-hand, with blank spaces reserved for the insertion of the name and style of the particular House for which it was made to serve, which in the present instance are supplied in a hand and with writing materials of a different kind. "To all the faithful in Christ," says this vile effusion, "to whom the present writing shall come, William Wyllyams, Prior of the Monastery or Priory of the blessed Apostles Peter and Paul of Taunton, in the county of Somerset, of the Order of S. Augustine, and the Convent of the same place, health eternal in the Lord. Know ye that we the aforesaid Prior and Convent, with unanimous assent and consent, &c., from certain just and reasonable causes"—which are, however, neglected to be stated—"specially moving our minds and consciences, have willingly and of our own accord given and conceded, and do by these presents give, concede, grant, and confirm to our most illustrious prince and lord Henry the Eighth, by the grace of God king of England and France, defender of the Faith, lord of Ireland, and on earth supreme head of the Church of England, the whole of our said Monastery or Priory of Taunton aforesaid, and also all and singular our manors, domains, messuages, gardens, curtilages, tofts, arable lands, and tenements, meadows, pastures, woods, underwoods, rents, reversions, services, mills, passages, knights' fees, wardships, natives, villans with their followers, commons, liberties, franchises, jurisdictions, offices, court-leets, hundreds, views of franc pledge, fairs, markets, parks, warrens, vivaries, waters, fisheries, ways, roads, void places, closes, advowsons, nominations, presentations and donations of churches, vicarages, chapels, chantries, hospitals and other ecclesiastical benefices of what kind soever, rectories, vicarages, chantries, pensions, portions, annuities, tenths, oblations, and all and singular our emoluments, fruits, possessions, inheritances, and rights whatsoever, as well within the county of Somerset, as within the counties of Devon, Dorset, and elsewhere within the kingdom of England, Wales, and the Marches, in any way pertaining, belonging, or annexed to the said Monastery or Priory." To this they add the gift of all their charters, evidences, writings, and muniments. All these possessions are given unreservedly to the aforesaid most invincible prince to use, dispose, alienate, grant, convert, and transfer, as shall be most agreeable to his royal will. The very same terms are used, in derision we may well suppose, as those which abound in the ancient instruments of saintly benefactors; and the pillaged and powerless victims conclude with the declaration that "the aforesaid lands with their appurtenances we by these presents will warrant to our aforesaid lord the king, his heirs, and assigns, against all the world for ever. In witness whereof we the aforesaid Prior and Convent have caused our common seal to be affixed to these presents. Dated in our Chapter House of Taunton aforesaid, on the 12th day of the month of February, in the thirtieth year of the reign of King Henry aforesaid." As if the seal were not sufficient, the signature of each of the community is thus added in the margin :—

"P' me Willyl'm Wyll'ms, P'or'.

P' me Will'm Gregory, Subp'orem ibm.

Thom's Mathen.
Wyll' Bayly.
P' me Nycolam Ber'm.
P' me Joh'nem Haywerd.
Thomas Dale.
P' me Will'm Culrun.
P' me Joh'nem Warryn.
P' me Willyelmu' P'son.
John Cokeram.
P' me Wyll'm Brynsmede."*

That man must be possessed of a hard and cruel heart, who can look at these signatures in the original document without emotion. The writer of the present lines can lay claim to no such apathy. To him these unsteady and hesitating characters are a most deeply affecting indication of agonized hearts and trembling hands, of a conviction that all that was dear was not only at the mercy of a sacrilegious tyrant but was gone for ever, of desolation and despair of soul from the knowledge that almost before those letters should have become dry the havoc and pillage would begin—that all that was left to them of their beloved and beautiful home was a wretched pension dependent on the caprice of implacable enemies, and that their future was a life-long wandering over a new and inexperienced world.

Nothing now remained but the destruction of the House and the division of the spoil. The very style and title of the place henceforth disappears, and it becomes "nuper Prioratus de Taunton modo dissolutus." Of the last scene I can furnish no memorial. No letter is known to exist of some sacrilegious commissioner recounting from Taunton

* Ex autograph. in Off. Rec. olim Augment. Appendix, No. CLXI.

his successive steps of heartless cruelty, nauseous hypocrisy, and impious wrong. There can be hardly a doubt that such was written, as similar were from Glastonbury, Fountains, Lewes, and a multitude of other places. And from these we may gain only too faithful a picture of the spectacle that was here presented. "I told yor lordshyp," writes one of these miscreants to Cromwell from the last mentioned locality, the great Priory of Lewes in Sussex, "of a vaute on the ryghte syde of the hyghe altare, that was born up wth fower greate pillars, hauing about it v chappelles, whych be compased in wth the walles lxx stokes of lengthe, that is fote ccx. All thys is down a Thursday & Fryday last. Now we ar pluckyng down an hygher vaute, born up by fower thicke & grose pillars, xiiij fote fro syde to syde, abowt in circu'fere'ce xlv fote. Thys shall down for o^r second worke. As it goth forward I woll aduise yor lordshyp from tyme to tyme; and that yor lordshyp may knowe wth how many men we haue don thys, we browght from London xvij persons, 3 carpentars, 2 smythes, 2 plummars, and on that kepith the fornace. Eu'y of these attendith to hys own office : x of them hewed the walles abowte, amonge the whych ther were 3 carpentars : thiese made proctes to vndersette wher the other cutte away, thother brake & cutte the waules. Thiese ar men exerciscd moch better then the men that we fynd here in the contreye. Wherefor we must bothe haue mo men, and other thinges also, that we haue nede of. . . . . At Lewes the xxiiij of March, 1537 (1539 ?)."*
"It would have made an Heart of Flint," writes a witness of a different stamp, recording the spoliation of Roche Abbey, "to have melted and weeped, to have seen

---

* MS. Cott. Cleop. E. iv. pp. 232, 233

yᵉ breaking up of yᵉ House, and their sorrowfull departing, & yᵉ sudden Spoil yᵗ fell yᵉ same day of their departure from yᵉ House. . . . . . The Church was yᵉ 1st thing that was put to yᵉ Spoil, and then yᵉ Abbat's Lodginc, Dortor and Frater, with yᵉ Cloister and all yᵉ Buildings thereabout within yᵉ Abbey Walls. . . . . It would have pitied any Heart to see what tearing up of yᵉ Lead there was, & plucking up of Boards, and throwing down of yᵉ Sparres, and when yᵉ Lead was torn off and cast down into yᵉ Church, and yᵉ Tombs in the Church all broken, ... and all things of Price either spoiled, carped away, or defaced to the uttermost."*

It is not improbable that on the very day that, as I believe, the former of these extracts was written a similar scene was exhibited at Taunton. The Surrender had been signed, as we have already noticed, on the 12th of the previous month; and we may be sure that it was not long before the demons of destruction were let loose to do their work. The demand for help just quoted, however, is sufficient proof that little assistance was obtained from the neighbourhood of the Monasteries. The agents of the tyrant had to bring abandoned and hardened ruffians from London to do their will and to execute their mandates. I need not attempt to draw more minutely the fearful picture of outrage, turmoil, blood, and fire. The walls which had for so many centuries resounded to the praises of God and the sounds of piety and learning were now invaded by a crew, whose very presence was a pollution and whose very aspect was a curse. The work of whole ages of faith and patience was in a few dreadful hours mercilessly destroyed and utterly ruined. But I forbear

* MS Cole, vol. xii., pp. 31, 32.

to enter further into their horror. The heart sickens while the blood boils at the imagination of the scene.

Such, doubtless, were the last hours of Taunton Priory.

The pittances which were ordered for each of the community are stated in a Pension Book, still existing among the documents of the Augmentation Office. The very grant of these pensions may be accepted as positive proof that the vices charged against the inmates of the Religious Houses were not only most grossly exaggerated, but were known by their accusers to be mere fabrications. Had the sufferers been really guilty, popular opinion would have allowed them to be sent adrift, even without this miserable concession to the known excellence of their lives and characters.

The entry referred to is as follows :—

"TAWNETON.—Herafter ensuyth the namys of the late p^{r}or and Covente of Tawneton in the countie of Som's' with the annuall pencons assigned vnto them by vertue of the Kinges highnes com'ission, the xij daye of ffebruary in the xxx^u yere of the reigne of o^r sou'eigne Lorde Kynge henry the viijth the furst payment of the saide pencons & cu'ry of them to begynne at the ffeaste of th' annunciacon of o^r blessid lady next comyng for one halfe yere, & so to be paide from halfe yere to halfe yere durynge ther lyffes—

that is to saye,

Will'm Will'ms p^{r}or	..	lx^{li}
Will'm Gregory	..	x^{li}
Will'm Baylye	..	vj^{li} xiij^s iiij^d
Nicholas Berame	..	vj^{li}

John Heywarde	..	cvj⁸ viij ᵈ
Thom'ᵉ Dale	..	cvj⁸ viij ᵈ and
the Cure of Saynt Jamys in Tawnaton		[s'uinge
to have for his yerly wages viij ᵈ accomptynge his pencon for p'te of the same.		
Thom'ᵉ Mathewe	..	cvj⁸ viij ᵈ
Will'm P'son	..	cvj⁸ viij ᵈ
John Waren	..	cvj⁸ viij ᵈ
Will'm Brunsmede	..	cvj⁸ viij ᵈ
Will'm Culrende	..	cvj⁸ viij ᵈ
John Cockeram	..	cvj⁸ viij ᵈ

Thom'ᵉ Cromwell.
Jo. Tregonwell.
Wylliam Petre.
John Smyth." *

In order to complete the history of these sorely oppressed and persecuted men, thus sent forth from their quiet home to brave the troubles of an unknown world, I would add that of the Prior and eleven Canons who signed the Surrender on the 12th of February, 1539, and received the pensions just enumerated, the following were living in the year 1553, as appears by a list then made. The same authority supplies us with the names of the last Incumbents of the Chantries in S. Mary's Church, and at Staverdale, by which it will be seen that some changes had taken place between the date of the Valor and that of the Dissolution.

"An. 1553, here remained in charge £6 13s. 4d. in Fees; £39 6s. 8d. in Annuities; and these Pensions, viz.:

To William Baylie, £6 13s. 4d.; Nicholas Besam, £6; John Warren, £5 6s. 8d.; John Hayward, £5 6s. 8d.;

* Pension Book, vol. 246, No. 164.

John Cockeram, £5 6s. 8d.; William Persons, £5 6s. 8d.; and to William Brynemede, £5 6s. 8d."

"Staffordell Chantry. To Robert Gulne, Incumbent, £5.

Taunton, St. Andrew's Chantry. To Henry Bull, Incumbent, £5.

Holy Trinity Chantry. To Ralph Wylkyns, Incumbent, £5.

St. Ethelred's Chantry. To William Callowe, Incumbent, £5.

St. Michael's Chantry. To John Seyman, Incumbent, £4 16s.

Virgin Mary's Chantry. To John Pytte, Incumbent, £4.

To William Trowbrydge, Incumbent of the Fraternity, £4.

To Alexander Maggott, Incumbent of Twing's Chantry, £3 14s. 4d."

And furthermore, William Callowe is stated to receive, as the Incumbent of a Service in West Monkton Church, an additional pension of £3 6s. 8d.*

We must now take up the history from the date of the suppression.

The difficulty was not entirely at an end, even when this defender of the Faith had appropriated the spoil. The lands lay as a heavy incubus on the spoiler. A curse was felt to be inalienably attached to them. People in general kept aloof, and refused to meddle with such dangerous property. The religious men of the day regarded the whole affair with loathing, and wisely forbore to involve themselves in the anathema which a participation in the wrong would attract. Even cautious men did not consider the purchase of such possessions in the light of by any

* Willis, Hist. of Abb., II. 200, 203.

means an eligible or safe investment. Accordingly, the domains which had in ancient times been given for the service of God and the benefit of the poor were squandered upon the lowest, the vilest, and the most abandoned of mankind. Greedy courtiers, renegades, mountebanks and miscreants of all descriptions alone benefitted, if so it may be called, by this wholesale sacrilege. And these new possessors were obliged to no exercise of religion, no work of compassion to body or soul for which the lands were originally bestowed. The stately portal with its right noble motto "JANUA PATET. COR MAGIS."* no longer, as of old, invited the wayfarer, and told him that, great as were its dimensions, the heart of its masters was greater still. No vesper bell sweetly whispered to the traveller that there were but a few steps between him and the welcome and repose that religion was glad to offer: no matin blessing dismissed him to his labours, and sent him once more on his way rejoicing and thankful. No aching bosom was henceforth there to be comforted, no wearied head to be laid to rest, no ignorance to be illuminated, no prodigal to be won to holier and better ways. They who, as these at Taunton, had so often received others of all sorts and conditions to hospitality and home, the King in his progresses, the great men of Church and State, the brother from some distant house, the displaced Monks of Buckland in the twelfth Century,† and the outcast and poor in every age, were now cast adrift that others might succeed by whom no such duties were held dear, and to whom mercy and charity would plead in vain. It was a foul wrong, without a single redeeming trait to set off its baseness.

---

* Monast. Dioec. Exon., p. 293.
† Monast. Angl. Lond. 1661, II. 650. Appendix, No. CLXII.

And it entirely fell short of the expectations of its designer,— pillage and persecution alone excepted. One even of the main objects of the king—who, it is pertinently said, "continued much prone to reformation, especially if anything might be gotten by it"—that, namely, of enrichment, suffered the most signal failure; and all this hideous work was within a few short months admitted to be of no service and to no purpose, though with its very perpetrator for a judge.

In order to facilitate the disposal of the estates, a new Survey and Valuation were taken. The former, so far as it has been preserved, relates but to a part of the entire property. It is, however a document of the greatest interest, as it furnishes the data from which the subsequent valuation was compiled, and has singular claims on the attention of the local reader. We are hereby presented with the minuter features of the several domains, which the return that was based upon it does not supply. I have accordingly given an analysis of it, which will make the detail that follows more intelligible; and the latter, usually called the "Ministers' Accounts," I have carefully compressed into a tabular summary.

The Survey, then—which seems, I may add, to have been preserved rather by accident than design—contains the particulars of the following estates, which are here placed in the order that they occupy in the original:—

1. The site of the Priory, with the Demesne Lands or Home Farm. The lands are enumerated together with their contents:—Carter's Mede, containing vj acr.; Carter's Lese, vj acr.; Avesham Mede, v acr.; Hole Mede, xxiij acr. The Seven Acre, vij acr. The Crofte, arable, xxxiiij acr. Hynde-londes, xxviij acr. The Crofte, meadow, x acr. More Close, vij acr. Caluen Lese, ij acr. A close next

the Day Howse, vj acr. Somer Lese, viij acr. Prie, iiij acr. The More, with pasture of wood, xiiij acr., and a close of arable land lying adjacent to a meadow called Seven Acres. Thre Acre, containing iij acr. The farm of the aforesaid amounting, with all and singular appurtenances, to the annual value of .. viij^{li} xviij^s x^d

2. The Grange of Barton or Blakedon. The lands are Barnchays-parke, containing j acr. Meade, ij acr. Oldeberes, iij acr. Orcharde, pasture, j acr. Flowre, x acr. Twent Acre Close, xx acr. Barnchayes, v acr. Seven Acker Close, vij acr. Woderofte, xij acr. Laushers, xij acr. A close lying next to Speryng, vij acr. Kyngeslease, xiij acr. A pasture near Laushere, j acr. Priors Parke. With all their appurtenances; together with vj^s viij^d of rent of a certain pasture in Lyng in the tenure of Thomas and William Blansheflowre; xj^s of rent of certain land in Pitmyster, in the tenure of Richard Milbury; and vij^s of rent of certain land in Pitmyster aforesaid, in the tenure of Thomas Speryng. The farm amounting to the value per annum of .. .. c^s

3. The Rectory of Corff and Pytmyster. The tithes of corn, pensions, portions, &c. according to the late valuation of a jury, deducting the stipend of a chaplain serving the cure there; amounting to the sum of .. viij^{li} vij^s The amount of the Chaplain's stipend, however, is not stated. It was probably the same as at the time of the Valor, when it amounted to c^s.

4. The Grange of Midelton. Oxenlese, containing xvj acr. A close next the Day Howse, ij acr. Howebonde Close, xvj acr. Trikeslande, viij acr. Middelle Graunge Close, xliiij acr. West Grunge Close, xl acr. Tenne Acres Close, xxviij acr. Combe Heys, xxx acr. Newe Downe Close, xl acr. Gotesland Close, xxvj acr.

Millchey, vj acr. Newe Medes, xxx acr. More Close, iiij^{xx} acr. Brokesmore Close, xij acr. The farm amounting to the value per annum of .. .. x^{li}

5. The Rectory of S. Mary Magdaline in Taunton, with the Chapels of Risshton, Trull, and Hull Bishop's.

Tithes of corn, wool, lambs, and other small tithes, deducting xx^{li} per annum for a pension to the Vicar; amounting to the annual value of .. .. ix^{li} xij^s xj^d

Similar tithes of the Chapel of Rissheton, deducting vj^{li} xiij^s iiij^d, for the stipend of the Chaplain there; amounting to the annual value of .. .. lxxvij^s xj^d

Similar tithes of the Chapel of Trulle, deducting vij^{li} xvj^d, for tithes of corn of Hamwod and Cerney, and vj^{li} xiij^s iiij^d, for the stipend of the Chaplain there; amounting to the annual value of .. .. lxvj^s viij^d

Similar tithes of the Chapel of Wilton, deducting cvj^s viij^d, for the stipend of the Chaplain there; amounting to the annual value of .. .. .. xxvj^s viij^d

Similar tithes of Hull Bishop's, deducting vj^{li} xiij^s iiij^d, for the stipend of the Chaplain there; amounting to the annual value of .. .. .. xj^{li} vj^s viij^d

The whole amounting to .. .. xxix^{li} x^s x^d

6. The Rectory of S. James's by Taunton, which would appear at this time to have become separated from and independent of the vicarage, with the Chapel of Stapelgrove.

Tithes of corn, wool, lambs, and other small tithes, deducting liij^s iiij^d, for the stipend of a Chaplain there; amounting to the annual value of .. .. ix^{li} xij^s xj^d

A note is entered on the margin, explanatory of the smallness of the Chaplain's stipend :—" M^d. that there was a Canon of the late Priorye there [Thomas Dale] com'ytted to s'ue [serve] the cure there, havyng therfor liij^s iiij^d by yere in augmentac' of his pencion as long as he wolde s'ue the sayd cure. Who nowe refusith to s'ue the same cure for soe small a stipend." The reader will remember in explanation of this note the memorandum appended to the list of the Canons' pensions at the period of the dissolution, already given in a previous page. Lower down on the same margin the very natural query appears "No^a. Who shall s'ue the cure here (?)"

Similar tithes of the Chapel of Staplegrove, deducting vj^{li} for the stipend of the Chaplain there; amounting to .. xl^s

The whole amounting to .. .. xj^{li} xij^s xj^d

7. The Rectory of Pytmyster, with the Chapel of Corff annexed to the same.

Similar tithes of grain, wool, lambs, &c., amounting to viij^{li} vj^s viij^d. The entry, however, is cancelled, as the item had already figured in the Survey under No. 3.

The sum total of the value as given by the return is lxxiij^{li} ix^s vij^d. And the declarations of its authenticity, correctness, and force are appended :—" ex^t p' Mathiam Coltch[irste?]," "fiat diss' John Ogan. Rychard Ryche."*

This account, though so circumstantial in the description of the localities, furnishes us with but little information on the value of produce, stock, wages, and other matters connected with the agriculture of that day or the history of prices. The land near the Priory, however, seems to have been estimated at about an average rent of xiij^d per acre ; while at Pitminster the average would appear to have been somewhat less.

We will now proceed to the summary of the "Ministers' Accounts," which were compiled, as we have already remarked, from the foregoing Survey and other similar returns :—

* Monasteries' Paper Surveys, in Off. Rec. vol. Zu. Appendix, No. CLXIII.

THE LATE PRIORY OF TAUNTON.
County of Somerset.

Taunton.
 The Site, with Demesne Lands .. viij^{li} xviij^s x^d

Esse.
 Rents of the Free Tenants .. xx^s
 Assised Rents .. .. xvj^{li} vj^s viij^d
 Farm of the Manor and Rectory .. xlvj^s ix^d
 Perquisites of the Courts .. viij^s v^d ob'

Westowe.
 Assised Rents .. .. vj^{li} iij^s iij^d ob'

Middelton.
 Assised Rents .. .. cxiiij^s vj^d
 Farm .. .. .. x^{li}
 Perquisites of the Courts .. c^s vj^d

Brewton.
 Rents of the Free Tenants .. xxxv^s j^d
 Assised Rents .. .. vj^{li}

Battecombe.
 Assised Rents .. .. xxxj^s
 Rents of the Free Tenants .. xv^s

Lovyngton.
 Assised Rents .. .. xliiij^s iiij^d

Thorncoffyn.
 Assised Rents .. .. iiij^{li} iiij^d
 Perquisites of the Courts .. v^s

Willond.
 Assised Rents .. .. xv^{li} ij^s iij^d
 Out Rents .. .. v^s x^d
 Perquisites of the Courts .. vj^{li} xvij^s x^d

Blackeden, &c.
 Assised Rents .. .. lxxvij^s xj^d

Berton.
 Farm of Grange .. .. c^s

CORFFE AND PITMISTER.
 Farm of Rectory .. .. viij^{li} vij^s
THURLOXSTON.
 Rents of the Free Tenants .. xiij^d
 Assised Rents of the Customary
  Tenants .. .. xiiij^{li} xiiij^s ix^d
PYXSTON.
 Assised Rents .. .. xv^{li} vj^s iiij^d
 Perquisites of the Courts .. xxiij^{li} viij^s iiij^d
TONRIGE.
 Assised Rents .. .. vj^{li} xviij^s ij^d ob.
 Perquisites of the Courts .. vj^{li} vj^d
CHAPEL OF WYLTON.
 Farm of Chapel .. .. vj^{li} xiij^s iiij^d
CANON STREET.
 Assised Rents .. ..xxix^{li} xviij^s iiij^d
 Perquisites of the Courts .. xx^{li} . viij^s iiij^d
TAUNTON EXTRA PORTAM.
 Assised Rents .. .. xiij^{li} iiij^d
 Perquisites of the Courts .. xlviij^s j^d
DULVERTON RECTORY.
 Rents of the Free Tenants .. x^s v^d
 Assised Rents .. .. x^{li} xiiij^s
 Farm of Rectory .. .. xj^{li} x^s
DULVERTON MANOR.
 Rents of the Free Tenants .. ix^s j^d
 Assised Rents of Customary Tenants xij^{li} ix^s vij^d
DULVERTON BAILIWICK.
 Rent called Downe Rent .. x^s
LUCOTT.
 Assised Rents .. .. xxxviij^s viij^d
DULVERTON.
 Rent called Shamellrent .. .. ij^s x^d
 Rent of certain Lands and Tenements iiij^s

WITHULL.
 Assised Rents   ..   ..   xxxjˢ

DULVERTON.
 Assised Rent called Bonvildes Rent   xxxijˢ
 Perquisites of the Courts   xxxiiij˪ˡ xviijˢ x^d
 Sale of Wood   ..   ..   xlvjˢ viij^d

GRASSCROFT.
 Rents   ..   ..   ..   xxxˢ

LANGPORT.
 Rents   ..   ..   ..   vˢ

ATHILBURY, OLDE CLIFFE, AND
 BRIGEWATER.
 Rents   ..   ..   ..   xxijˢ iiij^d

HOLCOMBE.
 Rents, and Rent called le Churchettes
  (a payment of corn as the first-fruits
  of harvest) ..   ..   ..   xvijˢ viij^d

TAUNTON HUNDRED.
 Tithe of xij Mills of the Bp. of
  Winchester   ..   ..   xlˢ

CLOWYNBARO.
 Pension from the Rectory   ..   iiijˢ

ORCHARDE.
 Pension from the Rectory   ..   vˢ

DULVERTON.
 Pension from the Vicarage   ..   lxˢ

LANGFORD, AND NEAR THE CHAPEL
 OF TAUNTON.
 Portion of Tithes   ..   ..   xiijˢ iiij^d

COURTHAY AND PRISTLONDYS.
 Farm   ..   ..   ..   xxiiijˢ

KYNGESHILL.
 Rents   ..   ..   ..   xlijˢ iiij^d

Fons Georgij.
  Assised Rents .. .. lxix^s x^d
  Perquisites of the Courts .. iiij^d
Galden.
  Assised Rents .. .. vj^u xij^s vij^d
  Farm of Lands, Tenements, &c. .. iiij^li
Thurlebare.
  Rents .. .. .. lxxvij^s viij^d
West Hatche.
  Rents .. .. .. xxxvij^s viij^d
Uppe Hatche.
  Rents .. .. .. xxiij^s iiij^d
Stooke.
  Rents .. .. .. viij^d
Thurlebare and Stoke.
  Farm of Rectory with Chapel .. ix^li xiij^s iiij^d
Hulle Bishop's Chapel.
  Farm of Tithes .. .. xviij^li
Withill.
  Farm of Rectory .. .. iiij^li vj^s viij^d
Staffordell.
  Farm of Manor House .. .. c^s
Wyncaunton.
  Assised Rents .. .. viij^li v^s
  Farm of Rectory .. .. viij^li
Roundhill.
  Farm of Manor House .. .. ix^li
Barowe.
  Assised Rents .. .. viij^li vj^s vij^d
  Perquisites of the Courts .. v^s viij^d
Kyngeston.
  Farm of Rectory .. .. xiiij^li
Taunton. Rectory of S. Mary Magdalene.
  Tithes .. .. .. xxix^li xij^s xj^d

TAUNTON. RECTORY OF S. JAMES.
 Tithes .. .. .. xij^{li} vj^s iij^d
STAPELGROVE CHAPEL.
 Tithes .. . .. viij^{li}
RYSSHETON CUM STOKE.
 Tithes .. .. .. x^{li} xj^s iij^d
TRULL.
 Farm of Rectory .. .. xv^{li}
PALLYNGEFORD, HOLFORD, & OTEFORDE.
 Farm of Tithe .. .. .. vij^{li} vij^s iiij^d
NYNEHED.
 Farm of Rectory .. .. vij^{li} *

A comparison of the values here given with those of the same localities as presented in the "Valor" does not offer, with the exception of one department, many cases of notable difference: indeed, in several instances the sums are identical. The exception is in the increase in the Perquisites of the Courts, which, for example, in Middelton are stated in the "Valor" to be vj^s viij^d, and in the "Minister's Accounts" to amount to c^s vj^d; and in Willond, Tobrige, Pixston, and Canon Street, to be respectively ix^s, xvj^d, iij^s iiij^d, and xxx^s in the "Valor," and vj^{li} xvij^s x^d, vj^{li} vj^d, xxiij^{li} viij^s iiij^d, and xx^{li} viij^s iiij^d in the later return.

We have now, in conclusion, to see how the spoil was divided.

Sir William Zouch has already been mentioned as the founder of the Priory of Staverdale. It appears that the possessor of the name at the period at which we have arrived was determined if possible to regain as his portion

---

* Comput. Ministr. in Off. Rec. olim Augment. Appendix, No. CLXIV.

of the prey the land which his pious ancestor had solemnly devoted to sacred use. He accordingly wrote to Cromwell, who was the king's principal agent in this work, the following characteristic letter:—

"Sure, pleshyt yo' good mast[er]chype to vnderston y' wer I dewlle ys a pore pryery, a fu'dacion off my nawynsetres, wyche ys my lord my father[es] yncrytans and myne, and be the reson off a lowyde pryor y' was ther, wyche was a schanon off taw'ton a for, browytte hytt to be a sell vnto taw'ton, and now hys hytt dystryde, and ther ys but to chanons, wyche be off no good leuyng, and y' ys gret petty, the pore howse scholde be so yll yntretyd; werfor yff ytt may plese yo' good mast[er]chype to be so good mast[er] to me to gett me the pore howse wyche ys callyd stau[er]dell, I wer bownde to pray for yo' mast[er]chyp. And also I schal bere yo" my harty s[er]uys nextt the kynge ys gras, and be at yo' co'-mayndme't, be the gras off god, ho eu[er] p[re]s[er]ue yo' good mast[er]chype. yo' howyne pore s[er]uantt and bedma',

RYCHARD ZOUCHE."

Endorsed:—"To the Ryght worchypfull & my synglar good mast[er], mast[er] Secrettory, be thys Dd." *

The two canons alluded to by the writer of this letter were the chaplains already mentioned in the Valor, whom it suited his purpose to revile. Although it does not appear that the epistle was productive of the precise effect that he desired, as the "fu'dacion off my nawynsetres" was granted to John, earl of Oxford, he is mentioned, as we shall see presently, in the Originalia roll as obtaining possession of divers lands, tenements, and messuages in the immediate neighbourhood.

* MS. Cott. Cleop. E. iv., f. 315. (Olim, 259*)

Several years elapsed from what appears to be the date of the foregoing letter, a fact which can hardly be accounted for save by our knowledge of the feeling with which the fruits of sacrilege were even then regarded, before the site of the Priory was formally transferred to other hands, when it was given by its new master to two of his creatures. On the 13th of June, 1544, the king granted to Sir Francis Bryan and Matthew Coltchirste all the house and site of the late Priory of Taunton, and all the messuages, houses, buildings, dovecots, pools, vivaries, gardens, orchards, arable and other lands, and inheritances whatsoever, situated and included within the site, enclosure, compass, circuit, and precinct of the same late Priory. Also all those arable lands, meadows, pastures, and inheritances whatsoever, called or known by the name or names of Carters Lease, Carters Meade, Avysham Meade, Seven Acres Meade, Hole Meade, Ley Meade, More Close, the Crofftes, Hynde Landes, Calfeven Lease, Somer Lease, Pry Close, More Close, and all the close next the Deyhouse; and all the close called Three Acres; and all those lands and woods called Priours Woode; and all other lands, meadows, pastures, woods, and inheritances whatsoever, commonly denominated and called the Demayne Landes of the said late Priory. These possessions are described as situated in Taunton, Hull Bishop's, Staplegrove, Russheton, Trull, Corff, Pytmyster, Churche, Hilfarance, Norton, Kyngeston, and Cheddon, and as formerly belonging and pertaining to the said late Priory. All these, with the produce of the woods, rents, yearly returns and all other rights, profits, and emoluments, are estimated at the clear annual value of eight pounds eighteen shillings and ten pence. They are stated to be granted in consideration of good, true, and faithful service—we need not stay to surmise its nature—rendered by these dutiful adherents; and the somewhat dubious favour is added of permission to hold the property as fully, freely, and entirely as the late owners had done, and to enjoy it as much as they. Finally, that the lands were to be held by them as tenants in capite, by the service of a twentieth part of one knight's fee, and an annual rent of seventeen shillings and eleven pence, to be paid at Michaelmas in every year: all profits and rents to commence from the Feast of the Annunciation last past. Witness the king at Westminster, the 13th day of June.*

Other portions of the property were given to various persons about the same time. William Chapleyn and John Selwood obtained, on the 5th of March, 1545, a grant of lands, tenements, gardens, cottages, and burgages situated outside the East-gate in Taunton, and in Canon Strete, Middel Strete, and Seint James Strete, in the parishes of S. Mary Magdalene, S. James, and Westmonkton. Also lands called Baldewynslande, and others lying near to Creechburgh Hill within the last named parish; land situated north of the Chapel of S. Margaret, then or lately in the occupation of divers poor people of the Spittelhouse there; land called Seint Poles Chapell in the west part of the said town of Taunton, in the parish of Hill Busshopp; and land called Seint Leonardes Chapell in the northern part, in the parish of S. James, all formerly belonging to the Priory.† To Alexander Popham and William Halley were granted lands in Thurlebare, West Hatche, and Upp Hatche, together with the messuage and tenement of Playstrete, and the manor and demesne of Tobrydge in

* Pat. 36 Hen. VIII., p. 21, m. 14 (38). Orig. 36 Hen. VIII., 6 pars, rot. 25. Rep. Orig. B.M. Add. MS. 6366, p. 90. Appendix, No. CLXV.

† Orig. 36 Hen. VIII., 4 pars, rot. 93. Appendix, No. CLXVI.

the parish of S. James's.* To Humphry Colles the Grange of Barton or Blakedon, with lands called Barnehayes, Parke-meade, Oldhayes, Orcheyarde, Twentie acres, Woodcrofte, &c., with the rectory and chapel of Corff and Pytmyster, and tenements in Catanger.† To John, earl of Oxford lands at Stafferdell, a Particular for the grant of which is dated 23rd Oct., 1543, and a "Certyfycat of the vewe and measure of ye woode," on the 13th of the previous June; and to Sir Thomas Arundell and Richard Zouche divers other lands at Staffordell.‡ To William Standyshe the manor of Gaulden, and other lands and tenements in Tollond.‖ To Robert Hyll the manor of Thurlebare, and messuages in Westbatche, Tobrydge, &c.§ And to William Eyre, lands at Nynehedde.¶ To pursue further the history of the various estates after the suppression would lead us into details, the value of which, as connected with our present subject, would not appear, although they possess a great and peculiar interest of their own, to warrant so considerable an expenditure of labour, space, and time.**

An exception may, perhaps, be made in favour of the sacred site of the Priory itself. Whether it was that Sir Francis Bryan and Matthew Coltchirste entertained some qualms about the nature of their perilous property must be left to conjecture. So early, however, as the year 1549, or about five years after their first acquisition of it, they pro-

* Orig. 36 Hen. VIII., 8 pars, rot. 17. Appendix, No. CLXVII.
† Orig. 34 Hen. VIII., 3 pars, rot. 32. Appendix, No. CLXVIII.
‡ Orig. 36 Hen. VIII., 7 pars, rot. 91. Appendix, No. CLXIX.
‖ Orig. 36 Hen. VIII., 8 pars, rot. 11. Appendix, No. CLXX.
§ Orig. 37 Hen. VIII. p. 1. rot. 40. Appendix, No. CLXXI.
¶ Orig. 36 Hen. VIII., 9 pars, rot. 51. Appendix, No. CLXXII.
** See 5 Edw. VI. Paso. Rec. rot. 1. 7 Eliz. Hil. Rec. rot. 40. 18 Eliz. Hil. Rec. rot. 86. 19 Eliz. Hil. Rec. rot. 99. 9 Jac. I. Mich. Rec. rot. 132, &c.

cured a licence for alienating it to one Thomas More.
The licence is dated at Westminster, the 22nd of June,
in that year, and recites the various possessions—Carters
Lees, Carters Meade, Avesham Mede, Hole Meade, Seven
acre Meade, Ley Meade, More Close, the Croftes, Hynde
Londes, Chalfeuenlease, Pry Close, More Close, the whole
close next the Deyhouse, Three Acres, the woods and
lands called Priours Woode, the lands commonly called
the Demeane Landes, situate in Taunton, Hull Bishop's,
Staple Grove, Rysshton, Trull, Corff, Pytmyster, Chyrche,
Hylfarance, Norton, Kyngeston, and Cheddon.* He and
his kept possession for a while, until in four short-lived
generations the family, which had a hard struggle for
existence, and often seemed on the point of annihilation
through failure of heirs male, succumbed at length to the
mysterious law of retributive justice, which had so many
examples in that dreadful time to give it solemnity, and,
as one would imagine, to force on the minds even of the
most unreflecting of mankind a deep conviction of its
terrible truth—and "the name was clean put out."

Grassy hillocks, as I have already observed, alone mark
the spot on which the House was reared. Not a pier of
the noble Conventual Church, not a capital of one of its
clustered columns, not a boss from the vaulted roof, not a
fragment of tracery through which the light fell in soft and
many-coloured radiance upon the chequered pavement, not
even the half obliterated lines of a sculptured slab that
once told of saintly Prior or learned Canon, who had gone
to his reward and left the memory of his virtues to devoted
and faithful hearts—not a solitary relic of that glorious
whole has escaped the hand of the relentless spoiler. All is

* Orig. 3 Edw. VI., 4 pars, rot. 05. Rep. Orig. B.M. Add. MS. 6367, p. 98.
Appendix, No. CLXXIII.

gone—and that it was ever there seems to the eye of sense
but a dream of the imagination, and a flight of fancy.
Yet amid its quiet and unbroken stillness there is a charm
that inalienably haunts the place, a magic that can
pourtray for us some fair lineaments of the sacred scene,
before evil hands invaded its repose and evil feet entered
to violate its peace. The eye of the soul can once
more picture the spot glorified as it was of old, and
peopled with the noble forms that blessed and dignified
their venerable and stately home. While the spirit's ear
can grandly realize the assertion of the legend, and induce
its possessor to believe, with the old neighbours from
whom I have listened to the reverently narrated account,
that, as he rambles among the green mounds, when all
nature seems asleep under the cloudless moon of a summer
midnight, he can hear the Canons still singing in their
Church beneath the dewy sward, and chanting their
solemn Office, at once an imploring deprecation of woe
to come and a requiem in loving valediction of days long
passed away.

www.ingramcontent.com/pod-product-compliance
Lightning Source LLC
Chambersburg PA
CBHW030313170426
43202CB00009B/984